The
Non-Designer's
Type
Book

The Non-Designer's Type Book

Insights
and techniques
for creating
professional-level type

Robin Williams

Peachpit Press
Berkeley ✷ California

The Non-Designer's Type Book
Robin Williams

parts of this book were originally published as
Beyond The Mac is not a typewriter

Peachpit Press
1249 Eighth Street
Berkeley, California 94710
800.283.9444
510.524.2178 phone
510.524.2221 fax
Find us on the World Wide Web at **www.peachpit.com**

Peachpit Press is a division of Addison Wesley Longman

Much of the information in this book was previously printed
in various articles in various magazines over the past few
years, including *Desktop Communications, Technique
Magazine,* and *Adobe Magazine.* The chapter "Telltale Signs
of Desktop Publishing" was originally printed in slightly
altered form in *Adobe Magazine,* July/August 1995 under
the title "Thirteen Telltale Signs." ©1995 Adobe Systems,
Inc., all rights reserved.

ISBN 0-201-35367-9

10 9 8 7 6 5 4 3 2 1

Printed and bound in the United States of America

To Allan Haley
with grateful appreciation
for inspiring, educating,
and befriending me.

I advise the layperson
to spread India ink
on an uncarved board,
lay paper on top of it,
and print it.
He will get a black print,
but the result is not
the blackness of ink,
it is the blackness of prints.

Now the object
is to give this print
greater life and greater power
by carving its surface.
Whatever I carve
I compare with an uncarved print
and ask myself,
"Which has more beauty,
more strength,
more depth,
more magnitude,
more movement,
more tranquility?"

If there is anything here
that is inferior to an uncarved block,
then I have not created my print,
I have lost to the block.

Shiko Munakata

Contents

Futuri
Baskerville

Typographic Choices 167

Other Info 211

*The trumpet don't make the music
and the computer don't make the type.
You can put a cat in the oven
but that don't make it a biscuit.*

Introduction ~

With the advent of computers on the desktops in the late twentieth century, type and typography reached new heights of popularity. With this increased awareness has come increased sophistication and the need for the average person to understand how to create beautiful, professional typography that emphasizes the message, typography that is pleasing to the reader, and that invites readers in and keeps them there.

If you have read and followed the guidelines in *The Mac is not a typewriter* or *The PC is not a typewriter,* you are already creating type on a more professional level than you were before.* This book takes you several steps beyond those basic guidelines, into even more subtle details that make the difference between good and sophisticated. You already recognize the difference—I'm sure you can glance at the two samples on the following page and instantly give an opinion as to which one is of higher quality. But can you name exactly what is creating that difference? Some differences are easily identified, others are more subtle. All are important.

If you're creating web pages, you'll find that many of the most important typographic techniques cannot be accomplished in the plain text on a web page. Type on the web will grow more sophisticated in the future, but for now many of the special techniques can only be applied to web pages as graphic pieces of type; that is, you create the headlines or fancy type in a graphics application, then put that graphic onto the web page. When you make that graphic text, you should of course apply every professional technique available.

Some of the guidelines in this book are too time-consuming to achieve for many everyday jobs, and I don't want you to think that unless you follow every suggestion here, your type will be inferior. But a key to creating great type is knowing what the options are in the first place. Once you know them, you can make choices as to when it might be appropriate to forgo some of the finer features.

So spend a couple of moments with the next few pages, make yourself conscious of the details, and see how many differences you can name before you look at the list. Then onward through the rest of the book, joyfully!

---

*Or if you read Beyond The Mac is not a typewriter, *then you don't need this book! This book in your hand is almost exactly the same as* Beyond The Mac is not a typewriter, *just a different title.*

Training your eye

Glance quickly at the two quotations set below, and be conscious of your instant reaction as to which one has a more sophisticated appearance. Then look more closely at the one on the left, and see how many details you can pinpoint that contribute to its unprofessional appearance. Then look carefully at the quotation on the right, and see how many differences you can spot. Each of those differences helps to create the cleaner and more sophisticated appeal of the second quotation setting.

"HUMAN SOCIETY, the world, man in his entirety is in the alphabet. The alphabet is a source...first comes the house of man and its construction, then the human body, its build and deformities; then justice, music, the church; war, harvest, geometry; the mountain, nomadic life and secluded life, astronomy, toil and rest; the horse and the snake; the hammer and the urn which--turned over and struck--makes a bell; trees, rivers, roads; and finally destiny and God.

That is what the alphabet signifies."
--*Victor Hugo*, 1802-1885

"HUMAN SOCIETY, the world, man in his entirety is in the alphabet. The alphabet is a source . . . first comes the house of man and its construction, then the human body, its build and deformities; then justice, music, the church; war, harvest, geometry; the mountain, nomadic life and secluded life, astronomy, toil and rest; the horse and the snake; the hammer and the urn which—turned over and struck—makes a bell; trees, rivers, roads; and finally destiny and God.

"That is what the alphabet signifies."
~*Victor Hugo*, 1802-1885

Wrong	**Better**
The 12-point type is large and clunky.	The 10-point type is easier to read because you can see entire phrases, plus it has a more sophisticated look. (p. 195)
The line length is too short to justify the size of the text, creating uneven word spacing and too many hyphenated words.	Setting the type flush left instead of justified ensures that there is even spacing between the words. (pp. 38, 119)
The quote marks are ditto marks, not true quotation marks. And the first "quote" mark makes the text appear to indent in the first line.	The quotation marks are true quote marks, and the first one is hung into the margin, eliminating the appearance of an indent. (pp. 53, 57)
The computer ellipsis (…) is too tight.	The ellipsis is set with thin spaces and periods for more elegant spacing. (pp. 66–67)
Double-hyphens are used instead of em dashes.	Em dashes are used instead of double hyphens. (p. 68)
The paragraph space is created by hitting two Returns, making much too much space between paragraphs.	The space between paragraphs is only half a line space, maintaining a closer connection between paragraphs. (p. 114)
There are two-letter hyphenations. And the last paragraph has the worst sort of widow (a hyphenated last word).	Hyphenations have been eliminated. (p. 144)
There is a hyphen between the dates instead of an en dash.	Oldstyle figures are used for the dates, separated by an en dash. The en dash is given a baseline shift downward. (p. 72)
The small caps are computer generated, creating a discrepancy between the stroke weights of the small caps and those of the other letters and the capital.	The small caps in the first line are true-drawn. (p. 87)
The byline (Victor Hugo) is italic, so the comma after his name should also be roman, not italic. (p. 67)	In the byline, an ornament has been used instead of a dash. (pp. 159–160)
*Technically, the phrase does not need quotation marks around it, but I wanted to display them. When more than one paragraph is quoted, the proper convention is to place quotation marks at the **beginning** of each paragraph, but only at the **end** of the **last** paragraph.*	Swash characters were used for the first letters of Victor Hugo's name. These are not only a subtle visual pleasure, but also prevent the italic V from bumping into the dot on the lowercase i. (p. 147)
	Auto pair kerning has been used, and manual kerning where necessary. (pp. 103–108) Where appropriate, ligatures have been used. (pp. 91–92)

BOLDNESS HAS GENIUS,
POWER,
AND MAGIC IN IT.

Goethe

Review

This book is meant to follow *The Mac is not a typewriter* or *The PC is not a typewriter.* Rather than repeat everything I wrote in those first books, I must assume you have read it and are following those basic typographic principles. But just in case you think you're ready for this book without having read the other, I am including here a brief review. If you answer no (**N**) to any of these points, please take a few moments to read *The Mac/PC is not a typewriter.*

Y N   I type *one* space after periods, commas, colons, semicolons, exclamation points, question marks, parentheses, and any other punctuation.

Y N   I *always* use true quotation marks (" "), *never* dumb ol' ditto marks (" ").

Y N   I *always* use true apostrophes (' not '), and I *always* put them in the right places.

Y N   I know the differences between hyphens, en dashes, and em dashes; when to use each; and how to type them.

Y N   I know how to use the Key Caps desk accessory on my Macintosh or Character Map on my PC to access special characters such as ©, ™, ¢, ®, or £.

Y N   I know how to place accent marks over the appropriate letters, as in résumé.

Y N   I know better than to *ever* underline text.

Y N   I *rarely* use all caps, and when I do it is certainly not under the mistaken assumption that all caps are easier to read.

Y N   I *always* avoid leaving widows and orphans on the page.

In this book I elaborate on some of the information that's presented in *The Mac/PC is not a typewriter,* but the material in this volume is very different from the previous books. If necessary, run down to your library, find *The Mac/PC is not a typewriter,* and take twenty minutes to get the gist of it. Especially if you're still typing two spaces after periods.

Robin

Anatomy of type

Before we begin, let's look at a few characters up close so when you read specific typographic terms throughout the rest of the book, you'll know what I'm talking about.

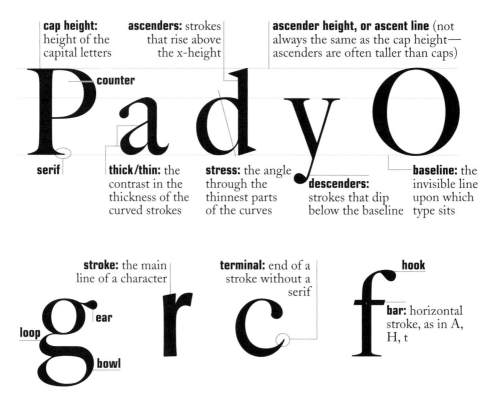

cap height: height of the capital letters

ascenders: strokes that rise above the x-height

ascender height, or ascent line (not always the same as the cap height—ascenders are often taller than caps)

counter

serif

thick/thin: the contrast in the thickness of the curved strokes

stress: the angle through the thinnest parts of the curves

descenders: strokes that dip below the baseline

baseline: the invisible line upon which type sits

stroke: the main line of a character

terminal: end of a stroke without a serif

hook

ear

loop

bowl

bar: horizontal stroke, as in A, H, t

SERIF
SANS

*Serif type has "serifs,"
as circled above. "Sans"
is French for "without,"
so "sans serif" type has
no serifs.*

a*a* f*f* g*g* h*h*
a*a* ff g*g* h*h*

Notice how the serif letter **a** changes from a "two-story" **a** into a "one-story" *a* when it is italic, but the sans serif does not. That is typical of how the design of most serifs and sans serifs change when italic (but not all).

body copy: text in sizes from about 8- to 12-point, set in paragraphs, as shown here (this is 10-point type).

display type: text in sizes above 14 point, as in headlines or advertising titles. Shown above is 90-point display type.

Roman means the type does not slant. This type is roman.

Italic type, *which does slant,* has been completely redesigned, as you can see by the comparisons (to the left) of the roman and italic versions of the same typeface. Most serif faces have true italic versions.

Oblique means the type is just slanted; this is typical of most sans serif "italic" faces (but not all).

The x-height

The x-height of a typeface is the size of the body of the characters as epitomized by the letter **x,** since x is the only letter that reaches out to all four corners of the space. It is the x-height that creates the impression of the font's size. You see, the point size of the type as you know it, let's say 24 point, originally referred to the size of the little piece of metal on which the letter was created. Within that 24-point space, the designer could do anything he wanted—he could make tall ascenders, a large x-height, a small x-height, short descenders. He didn't even have to take up the whole 24-point space. So when we say a typeface is a certain point size, we are really only getting an approximation of the actual number of points from the top of the character's ascenders to the bottom of its descenders. And even if the actual measurement from top to bottom is the same in several typefaces, the x-height varies widely. Since most of what you see of a typeface is the x-height, it is that which gives a face its visual impact.

Every one of the fonts shown below is set in 24-point type. You can see how radically the x-height changes the impression, even though most of the capital letters are relatively the same size. Be conscious of the x-height in the fonts you use—you will make some typographic decisions, such as linespacing, point size for body copy, and readability enhancement based on the x-height of the typeface.

These are all 24-point type.

Points and picas

When you're working with type, you need to work in points and picas. It's just like using inches and feet, but the sizes are smaller—there are 12 inches in a foot; there are 12 points in a pica. But like I said, points and picas are much smaller—there are 6 picas in 1 inch (which makes 72 points, then, in one inch).

Even if you've never formally worked with points before, you have a pretty good idea about how big 10-point type is as opposed to 24-point type because you choose and use point sizes of type on your computer all the time. So don't get nervous, just be conscious about those tiny sizes and try to use them more often. When your software, for instance, gives you a choice of using points or inches or lines, try using points. Once you start doing it, you'll probably find that it is actually easier to use points. I have a much clearer idea of how much space will be between the paragraphs if I ask for 6 points than if I ask for .083 inches. And I get confused about whether .083 inches is more or less than .072 inches, but I know darn well that 10 points is more than 8 points. Try dividing an 11-inch page into thirds. Ha! But change the measurement to picas, and the page is 66 picas, which is much easier to divide into thirds.

In general, we measure type sizes in points, and the space between lines or paragraphs in points. When measuring distances, such as the length of a line or the depth of a block of text, we use picas. Combining the two measurements is just like combining feet and inches: just as we write 6′2″ (6 feet, 2 inches), we write 3p4 (3 picas, 4 points).

Just so you know, traditionally (before desktop publishing) 72 points did not equal *exactly* 1 inch (it was a tiny smidgeon off). But when the Macintosh was created with a screen resolution of exactly 72 pixels per inch, our measurements for points became, on the Mac and then later on the PC, exactly 72 points per inch. Some software will let you override this standard, computerized amount and change it back to the traditional amount, but it's just about never necessary to do that.

A Brief History of Type

In which we briefly explore
the history of the world and
how it affects typography,
and how this in turn affects
your typographic choices.
Don't skip this chapter—
many references will be made
to the categories of type
as described herein.

Type is one of the most
eloquent means of expression
in every epoch of style.
Next to architecture,
it gives the most characteristic portrait
of a period and the most severe testimony
of a nation's intellectual status.

❧ Peter Behrens

Centuries of Type

The number of digitized typefaces is astounding, numbering well past 10,000 at the moment. It can be an overwhelming experience to decide which ones to buy, or even which ones to use.

However, if you group typefaces that have similar characteristics into a small number of categories, it makes the selection process much more manageable—it's easier to choose the typefaces you need to buy for your library by choosing a few from each category, and it's easier to decide which combination of faces to use on the page by making sure you grab no more than one from each category. And the process of grouping fonts makes you notice their more subtle features, makes you become more intimately involved.

It makes about as much sense to group several thousand faces into seven categories as it does to group human personalities into several character "types." There are always typefaces (or humans) with little quirks that prevent them from being conveniently pigeonholed, but there are generally enough shared characteristics to make it worth a try.

I'm going to talk about seven different categories: oldstyle, modern, slab serif, sans serif, fringe, script, and decorative. The first five groups follow a historical perspective—there are interesting parallels between type development and developments in other areas of civilization such as architecture, archeology, philosophy, even economics. This doesn't mean that every typeface in a category was developed at that point in history. Goudy Oldstyle, designed by Frederic Goudy in 1915, is a classic example of the oldstyle category which began developing around 1500. The printer Aldus Manutius is credited with cutting the first oldstyle type in 1495; in fact, Aldus was such an important character that I have reprinted a story about him at the end of this chapter.

Oldstyle

The characteristics of the oldstyle typefaces originally developed out of the traditional handlettering form, following the way the scribes held the pens and drew letters. When moveable type was developed in the mid 1400s, the letterforms that were carved out of metal resembled what everyone was familiar with—letters formed with a broad-tipped pen held at an angle. At that point in history, the only printed material was books. Big books. Books that sat on lecterns and were read aloud from. Since the only project for a printing press was to create books (there were no business cards or bread wrappers yet), the first typefaces were eminently readable because that's all they were supposed to be.

Oldstyle typefaces tend to have a warm, graceful appearance, and are the best choice for setting readable, lengthy bodies of text. Classic oldstyles are among the most "invisible," meaning that the character forms don't interrupt the communication; usually there are no design characteristics that trip your eye. The main body text for this book is set in a classic oldstyle called Caslon.

Oldstyle typefaces always have serifs. The serifs on the lowercase letters slant and are "bracketed," meaning the serifs connect to the main strokes with a curve. The strokes make a gentle transition from thick to thin, as the broad pen made naturally. And if you draw a line through the thinnest parts of the rounded forms of a letter, the line is diagonal—this is called the "stress"; oldstyle faces have a diagonal stress.

Caslon   Minion

Garamond

Bembo   Times

Palatino   *Oldstyle typefaces*

Modern

Times changed. The world changed. Type changed. Typefaces in the modern style were developed at a time when people were beginning to view the world differently. America ushered in democracy, France ushered out monarchy, the Industrial Revolution was underway, and political and social theorists were establishing a more rational, mechanical view of the universe and its inhabitants. Baroque, rococo, and oldstyle faces were rendered obsolete. Modern type reflected strict emphasis on structure and form, and the last vestige of type's handwritten origins disappeared.

Modern typefaces have a sparkle and an elegance, but they also tend to have a severe and cold appearance. They are not very *readable;* that is, they are not often the best choice for *lengthy* or small text, as the strong thick/ thin contrast creates an effect called "dazzling" that is hard on the eyes.

Modern faces have serifs, but the serifs on all characters are horizontal and very thin, with little or no bracketing (there is no curve where the serif meets the stroke). The strokes that create the letterforms change radically from thick to thin. The stress is now absolutely vertical.

Onyx   **Jimbo**   *Modern typefaces*

Bodoni

Bodoni Poster

Slab serif

Well, the Industrial Revolution really got going, and one of the results was a new field of business: advertising. Until then, of course, there were very few products to advertise. At first type designers tried to fatten up the thick strokes of the moderns, but the excessively strong combination of very fat strokes with very thin strokes made the text almost impossible to read. So they fattened up the entire letterform.

Slab serif typefaces also have serifs, and the serifs are horizontal, but they're thick. Fat. Slabs. The strokes that create the letterforms may make a very slight transition from thick to thin, or there may be no transition at all in some faces. The stress, when there is any, is vertical. Slab serif typefaces have a more regimented and strong appearance than do oldstyles.

I'll bet you were wondering why so many slab serif fonts are not named after their designers. Many of the oldstyle faces are named for their designers, such as Goudy and Baskerville and Garamond, but many slab serifs are named with Egyptian references such as Scarab, Memphis, Nile, and Glypha. It's indirectly because of Napoleon. One of his engineers found the Rosetta Stone, which turned out to be the key that unlocked the ancient hieroglyphics. This created a worldwide interest in Egyptian archeology and a mania for anything Egyptian. Type foundries noticed that if they named their typeface with an Egyptian reference, it sold better. To this day this category of type is sometimes called "Egyptian," even though there is no correlation between the style and the country except a fad. Slab serifs are also called "Clarendons" because the Clarendon typeface is the quintessential example of this category, as shown below.

Clarendon *Slab serif typefaces*

Memphis

New Century Schoolbook

Candida, **Candida Bold**

Sans serif

In 1816 William Caslon IV created a "two-line Egyptian" typeface in which he took off all the serifs because he hated slab serifs. This face was not a big hit. It wasn't until the Bauhaus school of design was formed in 1919 that sans serifs (typefaces without serifs; "sans" is French for "without") began to be popular. Under the Bauhaus motto of "form follows function," typefaces were stripped down to their bare essentials, to their simplest, most functional forms, epitomized in the font Futura. This new school of design influenced the world.

Sans serifs, of course, have no serifs at all. Also, the strokes that create the letterforms have almost no visible transition from thick to thin (there are a very few exceptions, such as the typeface Optima). Sans serifs tend to have very large x-heights and so present quite a presence on the page.

Futura: form follows function

Flyer Condensed   *Sans serif typefaces*

Formata   Trade Gothic

Fringe type

With the advent of the Macintosh computers and desktop publishing, type design—for the first time on earth—was put into the hands of the masses. More important than that, I believe, is that a mass *interest* in type was sparked—many people who never noticed typefaces before suddenly were wondering about the fonts on billboards and bread wrappers. With the power to create personal typefaces and to manipulate their layout on the screen, all the rules of traditional design and typography were demolished. Who knows where this typographic anarchy will lead to, but it is certainly fun and exciting to watch (and to use!).

Fringe typefaces (also variously called grunge, garage, deconstructive, edge, lawless, or just plain ugly) are typically distorted, schizophrenic, deliberately trashed, often difficult to read. But they are certainly identifiable and different from any other typefaces in history, and many are exquisitely beautiful in their ugliness. And they are incredibly fun to use. You might want to check out a fun book of mine called *A Blip in the continuum*, illustrated by John Tollett, that is simply a celebration of ugly type.

GLADYS

Fringe typefaces—aren't they amazing? I love them.

Marie Luise   Bad Copy

Amoebia Rain   fragile

Dirty One   THE WALL

Where's Marty?

Canadian Photographer

Scripts

Script and decorative typefaces have popped up in just about every period of typographic history. Script faces, of course, emulate handlettering in many varieties—blackletter (as in many of the Bibles handlettered by scribes), calligraphic (as in wedding invitations), drafting (as in architects' drawings), cartoon, and so on. No one has much trouble identifying typefaces in this category.

Isadora   *Script typefaces*

ExPonto Light   *Nuptial*

Carpenter   *Dorchester Script*

Emmascript   *Shelley Volante*

General Menou

Decorative

Decoratives are quite noticeable as well—the fonts made of ballet shoes or rope or Japanese pagodas or eraser dust. Decorative faces are not meant for anything else except to be decorative, which is far from an idle occupation. They can add punch to a publication, create a definite "look," or emphasize the content. If overused, they can destroy a design.

Bedrock   *Decorative typefaces*

Improv   **ChildrA DOS**

BILL'S FAT FREDDY

Le Chat Noir   **Mister Frisky**

Aldus Manutius

Have you ever wondered why roman type is called roman and italic type is called italic? Well, you can stop losing sleep over it.

Strange as it seems, in fifteenth century Italy, land of the Romans, very few publications were printed with Roman letters—almost all scholarly or religious works were set in *Greek*. There weren't many other sorts of books anyway, except scholarly or religious works. Not many romance novels or horror stories.

When the man Aldus Manutius entered the publishing business with his company called the Dolphin Press, the printing industry was less than fifty years old. But there were already more than a thousand presses operating across Europe, and literally millions of books had been printed. Aldus was proud and protective of his Greek fonts, but a bit sloppy and diffident about his Roman fonts. In fact, most of them were not very well designed, and he used them only for jobs sponsored by wealthy clients or academic friends. In 1496, though, Aldus published an essay for Pietro Bembo, an Italian scholar and friend. The Bembo typeface, with its lighter weight, more pronounced weight stress, and more delicate serifs, was an instant success. Claude Garamond picked it up in France and spread its influence throughout the rest of Europe. This "Aldine roman" typeface, Bembo, affected type design for hundreds of years. *(The body copy you are reading right now is set in Bembo.)*

Aldus himself produced well over 1,200 different book titles in his 25 years as a publisher. Over 90 percent of the books he produced were Greek classics. Aldus was a well-patronized scholar before he entered the printing and publishing trade, so the classics were close to his heart. The market for his books was made up of the educated, the worldly, and the wealthy. Aldus created small books, or *octavos,* intended for busy people, for nobility traveling across Europe on errands of state, and for members of the "educational revolution" who were studying in the growing number of universities. Thus Aldus was the first creator of small, portable, "paperback" books.

The official writing style of the learned and professional scribes of southern Italy in the late 1400s was a relaxed, oblique, and flourishy script called *cancellaresca*. To make his books more appealing to the higher-class market, Aldus took this exclusive writing style and developed a typeface out of it. It was a hit. What a marketeer.

Aldus had his new type style copyrighted. He was trying to protect not just the one font—he wanted a monopoly on the cursive sort of style. He got it; he even got a papal decree to protect his rights. But as we all know, that doesn't mean no one will steal it. People did. At least the other Italians called the style "Aldino"; the rest of Europe called it "italic," since it came from Italy. The first italic Aldus ever cut (well, actually Francesco Griffo cut it) was produced in 1501 in Venice. (Does the name "Venice" ring a bell?)

These innovations of Aldus Manutius place him in history as perhaps the most important printer of the Renaissance, next to Gutenberg himself. Popularizing the italic typeface, albeit inadvertently, had a profound influence on typeface development for generations. Prior to Aldus's beautiful octavos, the only small, portable books were prayer books; all other works were massive volumes that sat on lecterns for reading out loud. With the development of his italic type, more text could be set on a page, thus saving paper and space and making books more affordable. Education became more accessible, and the world changed. Again.

The function of reada-
        bility
  is often taken too liter
ally
anD over-emphasized at the
    cost of individuality.

                    Paul Rand

Readability and Legibility

In which we come to understand what makes type readable or legible, and how to improve the readability or legibility of typefaces in various situations.

HERE ARE THOSE WHO CONTEND that culture alone dictates our reading preferences, and that readability is based, not upon the intrinsic forms of the characters, but upon what we are *accustomed* to reading. Often cited as "proof" of this is the German preference for blackletter that continued centuries after the rest of the world had moved on to more sensible typefaces. Without proposing any scientific studies, I venture to suggest that just because someone *prefers* a particular typeface does not mean it is more *readable*. Your grandmother, I am sure, preferred that you send her a handwritten letter; in fact, she was probably offended if you wrote her a letter on a typewriter. Even though your type-written letter would have been easier to read than your handwriting, Grandma was not basing her preference upon readability, but upon other, more emotional responses. And I would propose that the German preference for blackletter was not because the letterforms were easier for them to read than what the rest of the world was reading, but that they had some other bonding with the blackletter forms.

Robin

Dear Grandma,
I wish you would let me use my computer to write to you. These darn letters take me two weeks to prepare. C'mon, this blackletter style is so old fashioned. Let me use one of my new and cool faces, like C h i c k e n ! It's easier to read than this silly font!

Love,
Sonny Boy

The Art of Readability

Readability and legibility are two key elements of printed text that typographers strive to maximize. **Readability** refers to whether an *extended amount of text*—such as an article, book, or annual report—is easy to read. **Legibility** (discussed in the next chapter) refers to whether a *short burst of text*—such as a headline, catalog listing, or stop sign—is instantly recognizable.

What makes a typeface readable?

There are several factors that determine whether text is readable. Most typefaces are either high or low on the readability scale simply due to the way they are designed. But a typesetter or designer can make any readable face unreadable, and conversely they can improve the readability of any face. It is your job to be conscious of both.

What makes a typeface intrinsically readable? Mostly it is a matter of a moderation of features, an invisibility. That is, whenever a feature of a typeface becomes noticeable, that face becomes slightly less readable. If a typeface has a very distinctive lowercase g, so distinctive that it makes you stop and say, "wow, look at that g," then it is lower on the readability scale.

Any part of the type that calls attention to itself—thick strokes, very thin strokes, a strong contrast between the thick and thin strokes of a letter-form, very tall and narrow forms, short and squatty forms, slanted characters, fancy serifs, swashes, or other extreme features—lowers the readability of the face because then you notice the letterforms rather than the message.

The most readable

The typefaces that make the most readable text are the classic oldstyle serif faces (remember those from Chapter 1?), either remakes of the original ones or new faces built on oldstyle characteristics. These typefaces were originally designed for long documents, since that's all there was in print at that time (late fifteenth to early seventeenth century). There were no brochures, advertising, business cards, packaging, freeway signs—there were only books. Big books. (In fact, it was Aldus Manutius, whose face you see still whenever you open PageMaker, who printed the first portable books in 1495.)

Other factors

Besides the distinguishing features of the typeface, there are other factors that can make text more or less readable, as described on the following pages. Once you are conscious of these factors, you can work with them to make even the least readable face more usable.

This is Belwe Light. Does your eye trip over the lowercase g or v or y? If your eye stumbles over the look of the type, it's not good for extended text.

This is Bernhard Modern, a very beautiful face, but too distinctive for extended readability. Great for brochures or other places where there is not an extended amount of text.

These faces have strong, noticeable features which make them quite distinctive. They are thus attractive for many uses, but there is too much distraction built into the faces to make them easy to read in extended text.

This is Minion Regular, a lovely font that was created specifically for lots of reading.

This is Garamond Book, also a lovely font that was created specifically for lots of reading.

Oldstyle typefaces have moderate features: there is moderation in the serifs, in the weight of the strokes, in the contrast between the thick and thin parts of the strokes, and in the x-height. I'll bet you can hardly tell these typefaces apart, right? It is this moderation, this lack of calling attention to the typeface itself, that makes oldstyles "invisible," which is ideal for communicating without an attitude.

Serif vs. sans serif

There are arguments about exactly why, but extensive studies do show that today in our society it is easier to read an extended amount of text when it is set in a serif typeface. Perhaps it is the serifs themselves that lead the eye from one character to the next, linking the letters into words. Perhaps it is the subtle thick-thin contrast in the strokes, which most sans serifs do not have. Perhaps it is the moderate ratio of x-height to cap height (the body of the letter in relation to the height of the capital letters or the ascenders), since sans serif letterforms tend to have larger x-heights.

Whatever the reason may be, accept the truth of it and use the knowledge in your typography.

Garamond Light, 10-point type

She had not gone much farther before she came in sight of the house of the March Hare; she thought it must be the right house, because the chimneys were shaped like ears and the roof was thatched with fur. It was so large a house, that she did not like to go nearer till she had nibbled some more of the left-hand bit of mushroom, and raised herself to about two feet high: even then she walked up towards it rather timidly, saying to herself, "Suppose it should be raving mad after all! I almost wish I'd gone to see the Hatter instead!"

Lewis Carroll, *Alice in Wonderland*

Formata Regular, 10-point type

She had not gone much farther before she came in sight of the house of the March Hare; she thought it must be the right house, because the chimneys were shaped like ears and the roof was thatched with fur. It was so large a house, that she did not like to go nearer till she had nibbled some more of the left-hand bit of mushroom, and raised herself to about two feet high: even then she walked up towards it rather timidly, saying to herself, "Suppose it should be raving mad after all! I almost wish I'd gone to see the Hatter instead!"

Lewis Carroll, *Alice in Wonderland*

Which of these feels easier to read? If you really want to use sans serif in your body copy, shorten the line length, add linespace, and use a smaller size type than for a serif.

Caps vs. lowercase

Text set in all capital letters (all caps) is more difficult to read. We don't read letter by letter—we read in phrases. When you see a word, you don't sound it out letter by letter, do you? No, you glance at the word, recognize it, and move on. A significant factor in our recognition of whole words at a time is the *shape* of the word. But when words are set in all caps, every word has a rectangular shape and we have to go back to reading the letters.

Now, although all caps are definitely more difficult to read, especially when there is a lot of text, sometimes you *want* the rectangular shapes of all caps. If that is an appropriate solution for your piece, do it freely. Just keep in mind that you are making a choice to exchange better readability for a design choice — sometimes it's worth it.

Temper this decision with the purpose of your piece. If you really need strength in readability, as in extended text (or in the case of all caps, more than ten words), or if you want people to be able to browse quickly as in catalog headings, a parts list, the phone book, a list of names and addresses, headlines, a table of contents, then don't use all caps!

Momma   Poppa   Sister   Brother

MOMMA   POPPA   SISTER   BROTHER

You can see how the shapes of the words in lowercase are so different from each other, helping us identify them. In all caps, all words have the same shape.

Is this word Momma, Poppa, Sister, or Brother?

Does this shape represent the word cat, dog, or garbage?

Letter spacing and word spacing

Again, since we read in phrases, uneven letter and word spacing disturbs our natural reading pattern; our eyes have to make constant adjustments between words. Spacing that is consistently too close or too far apart also disturbs our reading. There is no perfect rule that will fix the spacing for every typeface and every project—you must simply learn to see more clearly and then *trust your eyes*. If it looks like the words are too close together, they are. If it looks like the letters are too far apart, they are. Once you recognize appropriate and inappropriate spacing, you have the responsibility of learning exactly how your particular software controls the letter and word spacing. Ha! Read that manual.

Many script faces have connecting letters that need slightly *tighter* letter spacing so their letters will actually connect, but they also often need *extra* word spacing because the tails of the letters bump into the spaces between the words. Again, I cannot emphasize enough that you need to know how to control the spacing in your page layout application! (Most word processors do not have features to control the letter spacing.)

You are guaranteed to get terrible word spacing if you justify text in a narrow column, so don't do it. How do you know if it's too narrow? Read the following page.

It isn't what I do, but how I do it.

It isn't what I say, but how I say it.

And how I look when I do it and say it.

Mae West

So which one of the lines above is too tight? Which one has too much word space? Which one looks okay? See how good you are at this already? Trust your eyes.

Line length and justification

If a line is too long, we have trouble finding the beginning of the next line. If a line is too short, it breaks up those phrases we recognize. If you try to justify your type on a short line, you will get awkward word spacing and rivers. So how do you know what's a decent line length?

There are several rules of thumb to determine this measure. Some people suggest no more than nine to ten words on a line as a maximum, or no more than 2.5 times the alphabet, which is 65 characters. The rule I find easiest to remember for an optimum line length (mimimum for justifying) is this: Double the point size of your type, and use a line length no longer than that in picas. Say what? Well, let's say your type size is 9 point—your line length should be 18 picas. If your type is 24 point, your line length should be 48 picas. All you have to remember is that there are 6 picas in one inch: thus 18 picas is 3 inches; 48 picas is 8 inches. (Did you read page 18 about points and picas?)

Don't justify any text if your line length is shorter than this minimum! If you're using a classic, readable oldstyle and you really want it justified but you find that the word spacing varies too much even on this line length, make the line a few picas longer and perhaps add a tiny bit more linespace.

Figure out your optimum line length and then analyze your typeface. Shorten the line length of *non-justified* text for these reasons:

- If the typeface has a very large x-height or a very small x-height.
- If the typeface is a sans serif.
- If you are reversing the type out of a background or solid color.
- If the typeface is script, decorative, or at least rather odd.
- If you are presenting type where it is difficult to read, such as on a presentation slide or on a web page.

Linespacing (leading)

Linespacing is, obviously, the space between the lines. You have total control over how much space appears. Linespacing that is too tight decreases readability because it makes it difficult for the reader to separate the individual words and phrases, and it also makes it more difficult for the reader's eyes to find the beginning of the next line.

You will generally need to **increase linespacing** for these reasons:

- If the line length is longer than average.
- If the typeface has a large x-height, as most sans serifs do.
- If you are reversing the type out of a background or solid color.

You can **decrease linespacing** on an average line length if your typeface has a very small x-height since the small x-height creates more space between the lines naturally. But often when using a distinctive typeface with a small x-height, it is nice to reinforce that airy, open feeling by actually adding more linespace. See Chapter 15 on linespacing for more details and specific examples.

My way is and always has been to obey no one and no thing except that reasoning which seemed best to me at the moment when I made my decision. Never judge past action by present morality.

Socrates

The paragraph above is set with the default linespacing (leading) value. Notice it seems a little tight between the lines. Typeface is Formata Light.

My way is and always has been to obey no one and no thing except that reasoning which seemed best to me at the moment when I made my decision. Never judge past action by present morality.

Socrates

Just adding one point of space in the paragraph above helped to open up the text so it is more pleasant to read. Sometimes all you need to add is half a point; sometimes you'll need to add several extra points.

Reverse type and light or heavy weights

White type on a dark background (reverse) appears to be smaller than black type on a white background. Compensate for this by using a slightly heavier typeface and slightly larger point size (this is a great place to take advantage of multiple masters; see Chapter 30).

Which type appears smaller? **Which type appears smaller?**

Never reverse a typeface that has delicate features— very thin lines and tiny little serifs will clog up with ink and disappear. Doesn't this look awful?

The same guideline applies for text that is dropped out of a graphic image. I know it looks really great on the screen, but when ink hits absorbent paper, all kinds of havoc is wreaked upon unsuspecting delicate type. Don't let your work look foolish by ignoring the realities of the reproduction process.

Extra bold type and extra light type are also less readable than a regular weight face. If you use them, be sure to compensate—you may need extra letterspace, extra linespace, a bit larger or smaller point size. Your eyes will tell you what is necessary.

On **web pages,** avoid using colored text on a dark background. If you must, enlarge the size of the type a wee bit, and don't use bold or italic except in small doses.

Italic or script

Italics and scripts are more difficult to read in general because of their tight spacing, their curves and slants, their approximations to handwritten letterforms. Don't ever use them for extended text or no one will read your work. Maximize their readability:

- *Pay close attention to their letter and word spacing.*
- *Increase their linespacing if necessary.*
- *Make the line length shorter than average.*
- *Don't reverse them unless they are set in a relatively large size.*

Do you find this section less readable, even in this small amount of copy? Yes, these things are true—I am not just making them up.

Moderation is the key

I'm sure you see the pattern by now—moderation in every facet of typography is the key to eminent readability. Now, this does not mean that you have to be dull and boring and moderate at all times! It just means that you need to be conscious and make conscious choices.

- Perhaps you want to use a very distinctive face in a brochure. If the face itself is not intrinsically readable, then make up for it in other areas of readability—an appropriate line length and word spacing, avoid all caps, etc. Make sure that all other text is eminently readable, and then you can get away with areas of fancy type.

- If you want to use a sans serif in body copy, use a shorter line length and a little extra space between the lines.

- If you want to reverse text, make it a bit bolder and larger, and don't use a fine-featured typeface that has tiny little serifs or thin lines that will disappear.

- Save extra bold and italic and extra light for accents.

- If your typeface has an extra-large x-height, use more linespacing. If it has very tall ascenders, you can use less linespacing.

- If you're setting a book, manual, magazine, or other lengthy text, including a lot of text on a web page, use the most readable face in all its moderation. Save the distinctive faces for chapter titles, headlines, subheads, poetry, etc.

THROUGH TYPOGRAPHIC MEANS, the designer now

presents, in One image, both the message and the pictorial idea. Sometimes, this "playing" with type has resulted in the loss of a certain amount of legibility. Researchers consider this a deplorable state of af-fairs, but on the other hand, the excitement created by a novel im-age sometimes more than compensates

for the slight

DIFFICULTY

in readabil-ity.

Herb Lubalin

The Art of Legibility

Readability, as discussed in the previous chapter, refers to whether an extended amount of text—such as an article, book, or annual report—is easy to read. **Legibility** refers to whether a short burst of text—such as a headline, catalog listing, or stop sign—is instantly recognizable.

There have been extensive studies on type to determine which factors influence different aspects of reading, such as reading speed, retention of information, recognition of letterforms, etc. Interestingly, these studies show that in our culture and in our era, serif typefaces are easier to read when there is a lot of text, but sans serif letterforms are more instantly recognizable when there is a small amount of text. Sans serif characters tend to be direct and clear, with no serifs to add unnecessary tidbits to the shapes. When we read a large body of text, however, those same serifs help to guide us along the lines.

We don't read letter by letter; we see the entire word or the phrase and it goes straight to our brains. When text is less than perfectly legible, we have to spend extra time to read it. Sometimes this is only a split second, sometimes it's a more significant struggle, but it can make a big difference in whether the information is absorbed or tossed aside.

Text needs to be most legible (as opposed to readable) in situations where people are scanning pages, reading signs, or skimming through catalogs or lists—wherever they need to instantly recognize words without having to spend extra seconds to read them. For instance, in a newsletter, the headlines should just pop right off the page into the reader's brain. In a parts list, the reader should be able to slide down the page, absorbing the names of parts. In a table of contents, a reader should be able to scan the contents. Street signs, "Warning," "Danger," and all freeway signs should be instantly recognizable.

What are you saying?

Always be conscious of the words themselves. Some words, such as "Sale," can probably be set in just about anything and people will get it. But if you have an unusual name, don't set it on your business card in a typeface that is difficult to read! If words are long or foreign and extremely important, be especially careful to choose a typeface with great legibility.

What makes type legible?

Not all sans serif typefaces are eminently legible. One of the keys to legibility is the clarity of the letterforms, or how easy it is to distinguish one character from another. For instance, the typeface Hobo eliminates the descenders (see below); this is useful in certain applications, but it is not what we are accustomed to and thus this feature decreases its legibility.

I don't make jokes. I just watch the government and report the facts.
Will Rogers

Legibility depends on the instant recognition of letterforms.
When characters have odd shapes, we don't recognize them instantly.

Large or small x-height

An exceptionally large x-height decreases legibility. Some faces have such large x-heights that an "n" is hardly different from an "h."

And a very small x-height also decreases legibility. The body of the character is disproportionate to the cap height, and our eyes find this to be distracting—besides the fact that the letters appear too small.

I dote on his very absence. William Shakespeare

Notice there is not much difference between the "n" and the "h," nor between the "i" and the "l" in "William." Typeface is Antique Olive Roman.

Hercules himself could not beat out his brains, for he had none. William Shakespeare

Although this typeface is pretty and very distinctive, it is not the most legible. Typeface is Bernhard Modern.

Weight and proportion

✺ **Extra-heavy or extra-thin weights are less legible. A good solid bold, however, as long as it is not extra-heavy or condensed, can enhance legibility by giving a substantial contrast to the rest of the text. For instance, headlines are great in bold because the contrast of their weight attracts attention against the background of gray, readable text. But how do you like reading even this short paragraph in an extra-bold face (Antique Olive Compact)?**

✺ A monospaced font (such as Courier) creates inconsistent letter and word spacing, which makes it less legible (and less readable) because our eyes have to keep adjusting to the differences in spacing. Some faces are so poorly spaced that words can be misread at a glance.

✺ Using the computer to compress the typeface distorts its proportions and makes it less legible. If you want a compressed face, buy a specially designed font. See Chapter 12 for details and more examples on this topic.

All caps or
mixing caps and lowercase

▪ Mixing Lowercase And Caps In The Same Sentence Makes Type Less Legible *And* Less Readable. Your Eyes And Brain Have To Figure Out What's Going On Because We Are Not Accustomed To Reading This Way. This Is Called Title Case And Is Meant For Titles, Not Headlines Or Sentences.

Killing time takes practice. Karen Elizabeth Gordon

This typeface, Peignot, is interesting but not particularly legibile.
Or readable. It mixes caps and lowercase in the middle of words,
confusing our pea brains.

▪ WORDS SET IN ALL CAPS ARE THE LEAST LEGIBLE OF ALL, NO MATTER WHICH TYPEFACE YOU USE. MANY PEOPLE THINK IF YOU SET TYPE IN ALL CAPS IT IS BIG-GER AND THEREFORE EASIER TO READ. Wrong. We recognize words by their shapes as well as by their letters. Set in all caps, all words have the same shape. Have you heard this before?

In Washington, D.C., the streets have long names.
The street signs are set in all caps, squished to fit into
the standard green shape. Consequently, you must get
very close to a sign to tell what it says. If the street
names were in upper- and lowercase, you would be
able to tell Independence Avenue from Constitution
Avenue long before you could actually read the letters.

The most legible type

To make your text the most legible, use:

- A plain sans serif with an average x-height.
- A regular or medium weight (sometimes bold when appropriate).
- Lowercase letters (plus capitals where they belong).
- Not condensed or expanded or oblique (slanted).
- A little extra letter spacing in small point sizes (below 10 point); less letter spacing in large sizes (above 14 or 18 point).

Which of the following type samples is the most legibile?

1. **Few forgive without a fuss.** Hobo

2. *Few forgive without a fuss.* Ex Ponto Light

3. Few forgive without a fuss. Antique Olive Roman

4. Few forgive without a fuss. Schablone Rough

5. **Few forgive without a fuss.** Peignot

6. Few forgive without a fuss. Trade Gothic

7. Few forgive without a fuss. Bernhard Regular

Answer: 6, Trade Gothic
Can you see why?

Temper the rules with choice!

Now, please remember that these guidelines do not mean you should never use certain typefaces or formatting! It just means you must look carefully at your typeface and make a conscious choice—if your piece requires a high level of legibility, watch for the danger signs. If your job is one that people can take a tiny bit longer to absorb, or if the words are not unusual, then feel free to play with features that are not at the top of the legibility list. Use that beautiful face with the tall ascenders and small x-height for a sign, or that lovely, graceful script for a special title, or that extra-bold face for web page headlines. People can *read* it, of course. Know the guidelines, be conscious of your typeface and your purpose of communication, and make clear decisions based on knowledge.

And don't forget Herb Lubalin's theory, as presented on page 42. Lighten up and smile.

No passion in the world is equal to the passion to alter someone else's draft.

H.G. Wells

Punctuation

In which we explore
quotation marks and prime marks,
hanging punctuation,
optical alignment of characters,
punctuation style,
and baseline shift
for hyphens, dashes,
and parentheses.

I OFTEN QUOTE MYSELF.
IT ADDS SPICE TO MY CONVERSATION.
GEORGE BERNARD SHAW

Quotation Marks & not Quotation Marks

If you are choosing to read this book, you are probably already conscious of the difference between typewriter quote marks (" ") and true quotation marks (" "), often called "curly quotes" or "smart quotes." But let's make sure you are also using single and double prime marks where appropriate, and leaving the ditto marks in their place.

First, review of quotation marks and apostrophes

Most software has a checkbox called something like smart quotes, true quotes, typographer's quotes, or a similar phrase, like one of these:

☑ **Use typographer's quotes**

☑ Smart Quotes (' '," ")

Replace
☑ "Straight quotes" with "smart quotes"

If you check that box, the software will automatically insert true quotation marks when you type the " key on the keyboard. You will also get a true apostrophe when you type the ' key on the keyboard, as displayed below:

"No, don't do this."   "Yes, isn't this better?"

But be careful—if you trust the computer to always put the correct mark in the correct place, you will find people snickering at your work. For instance, when the automatic feature is on you will get quotation marks where you need inch and foot marks, like so: Bridge Clearance 12'6". Or when you have a quotation mark that appears right after a dash—"like this"—the quote mark goes the wrong way!

You need to know the key combinations to type the correct single and double quotes, both opening and closing, for those times when your software doesn't do it correctly. See the charts in Appendix C.

Don't embarrass yourself

Follow these basic rules so your work doesn't look dumb:

- Quotation marks at the beginning of a word or sentence are *opening quote marks* and curl *toward* the text (").

  Quotation marks at the end of a word or sentence are *closing quote marks* and curl *toward* the text (").

  These are often called "sixes and nines" because the opening marks are shaped like sixes and the closing marks are shaped like nines.

- An apostrophe belongs where a letter is missing, as in **cookies 'n' cream** or **rock 'n' roll.**

  Notice your computer automatically inserts a *backwards* apostrophe at the beginning of a word! For instance, your computer will do this: **cookies 'n' cream.** This is WRONG! And dumb!

  Know the keyboard shortcut to insert the correct mark:

To type this:	Mac	Windows
opening single quote '	Option Shift]	Alt 0145

- The word **it's** with an apostrophe means *it is* or *it has.* **Always.** Really and truly **always.**

  The word **its** *without* an apostrophe is the possessive form of the word, as in *hers, his, theirs,* or *its.* Notice none of those possessive words contains an apostrophe. *Don't put an apostrophe in **its** unless you mean **it is** or **it has**!*

- When talking about decades, such as **in the '90s,** there is an apostrophe where the other numbers are missing.

  Make sure you set an apostrophe and not an opening single quote! The phrase should not look like this: **in the '90s,** which is what you will get if you let the computer type it for you.

  Also notice there is no apostrophe before the s (not **in the '90's,**) because generally you are referring to a plural number of years, not a possessive number.

Single and double prime marks

Another problem with letting your computer automatically type the quotation marks for you is that you end up with quotation marks and apostrophes when you really need inch and foot marks.

Wrong: **Jenifer stands 5' 8" tall.**   Right: **Jenifer stands 5'8" tall.**

Now, you might think that you should be typing those ugly typewriter apostrophes and quotation marks for inch and foot marks. Wrong, dear. In excellent typography, feet and inches are represented by single and double *prime marks,* which are at a slight angle, as shown below.

These are typewriter quote marks: **" '**

These are double and single prime marks: **″ ′**

If you have the Symbol font on your computer (which you probably do), you can use the prime marks in it:

To type this:		Mac	Windows
single prime mark	′	Option 4	Alt 0162
double prime	″	Option Comma	Alt 0178

However, it's very possible that the prime marks in the Symbol font do not match the weight of your characters. Until every font has prime marks built in, you might often have to use the italic version of your typewriter apostrophes or quotations marks, as shown below.

Using the Symbol font here looks silly: **Jenifer stands 5′ 8″ tall.**

Use italic typewriter marks: **Jenifer stands 5'8" tall.**

Technically, prime marks are not meant specifically as inch and foot marks, but as markers of divisions of equal parts. For instance, you would also use the single prime mark to show the minutes or degrees of an angle or a turn, as in 12° 8′ (read 12 degrees and 8 minutes).

Ditto marks

So what good *are* those characters on your keyboard? Well, go ahead and use them in e-mail because it's too much trouble to take the time to set real quotation marks. And until every browser used on the World Wide Web can interpret the code correctly, we are stuck with typewriter apostrophes and quote marks there. You can use these as ditto marks, should you ever need to set ditto marks to show that an item is repeated, as shown below (although some people do prefer to use double prime marks as ditto marks).

Superman	128 Power Street	Metropolis	USA	
Lois Lane	327 Reporter Way	"	"	——— *ditto marks*

A helpful chart

In case you are still confused, here is a little chart that sums up the wrongs and the rights. Find the phrase that matches what you want to say and follow its example.

Wrong	Why it's wrong	Right
Food at it's best	The phrase does *not* say, "Food at it is best."	Food at its best
In it's shell	The phrase does *not* say, "In it is shell."	In its shell
Where its at	The phrase says, "Where it is at."	Where it's at
Hall 'o' Fame House "O" Glass	The "f" is missing from "of." There is nothing missing in front of the letter "o."	Hall o' Fame House o' Glass
Gone fishi'n	The "g" is missing.	Gone fishin'
Rock 'n' Roll Rock 'n Roll Rock n' Roll Rock 'n Roll	Both the "a" and the "d" are missing from "and." So an *apostrophe* belongs where each letter is missing—an *apostrophe,* not an opening single quote mark!	Rock 'n' Roll Rock 'n' Roll Rock 'n' Roll Rock 'n' Roll
In the 60's (decade)	This is not possessive, it is plural. The "19" is missing from "1960."	In the '60s

5 Hang that Punctuation

Using real quotation marks and apostrophes is a good sign that you've progressed beyond typewriter mentality. Now that you're using the correct punctuation, the next step is to hang it (where appropriate).

What does it mean to hang the punctuation? Well, take a look at the quotations below. In the left one, would you agree that the first line appears to be indented? Obviously, it is the empty space below the quotation mark that creates that illusion. Take a look at the same quotation on the right. Now the left edge of that text has a strong, clean alignment, and the punctuation is "hanging" outside that edge. That clean edge is what you want; it is a sign of being conscious of your typography.

"What you do
speaks so loudly
that I cannot hear
what you say."

Ralph Waldo Emerson

"What you do
speaks so loudly
that I cannot hear
what you say."

Ralph Waldo Emerson

You can easily see, in the example on the left, what a visual gap the quotation mark creates. Hanging the punctuation off the edge of the text maintains the strong, clean alignment. Typeface is Eurostile Demi.

When to hang it

Punctuation should always be hung when type is set aside from the main body of text or when set large, as in a quotation, pull quote, headline, poster, etc. If the type is set flush right, the periods or commas at the ends of the lines should also be hung if they interrupt the right edge of the type. (Except in very fine typography, punctuation in body text is usually not hung because of the trouble it takes and because the interruption in the line is not as significant when the type is small.)

"I'm laughing
at the thought
of you laughing,
and that's how laughing
never stops in this world."
Zorba the Greek

"I'm laughing
at the thought
of you laughing,
and that's how laughing
never stops in this world."
Zorba the Greek

I'm sure you agree that both of these pieces of type need the punctuation hung.

"I'm laughing
at the thought
of you laughing,
and that's how laughing
never stops in this world."
Zorba the Greek

"I'm laughing
at the thought
of you laughing,
and that's how laughing
never stops in this world."
Zorba the Greek

Oooh, look at those nice clean edges. The strength of that edge gives strength to the page. Typeface is Eurostile Demi.

Optical alignment

The point of hanging the punctuation is to keep a strong left or right edge. Often this means aligning the edge with a stem (vertical stroke) rather than with a bar (horizontal stroke), as in the letter "T." Align the second line of type with whatever is the strongest edge of the initial character you see—remember, your eye is always right! *If it doesn't look aligned, it isn't.* You might have to align with the bottom point of the capital "V," or just inside the outside curve of an "O." Whichever part of the letter is the closest or most obvious visual connection, align with it. This is called "optical alignment" because you are not aligning by a ruler, but by your eye.

"You believe easily that which you hope for earnestly."

Terence

Even though the top edge of the letter "Y" is aligned with the second line of type, it still appears to be indented. That's because our eyes see the vertical stem of the "Y," rather than the top angle, much more closely related to the "t." Typeface is Eurostile Demi.

"You believe easily that which you hope for earnestly."

Terence

Above, the stem of the "Y" is aligned with the "t." This is an optical alignment rather than a measured alignment.

Just how do you hang it?

At first, hanging punctuation might seem like a silly task. But as your typographic consciousness is raised, I guarantee you will also begin to see hung punctuation as a sign of professional type. There are several methods of doing this, depending on the project and the software.

Use an indent

One of the easiest ways, if the quote is a paragraph on its own and is flush left, is to use an indent, as shown below. If you use this setup regularly in your publication, make a style sheet for it.

Set your indents so the first line marker is flush left, and the left indent marker is aligned along the stem of the first letter.

"It's as large as life and twice as natural,"
said Alice.

Use hard spaces

A "hard space" is an empty space that is different from the regular space that you type with the Spacebar. A hard space doesn't "break" like a regular word space does—a non-breaking, hard space connects two words as if they were one word. For instance, to prevent the name "Ms. Scarlett" from breaking into "Ms." at the end of one line and "Scarlett" at the beginning of the next line, you would type a hard space between "Ms." and "Scarlett," and then the phrase "Ms. Scarlett" would never break into two words

You can indent on the left or right with hard (non-breaking) spaces, if your software allows it (try it and see). Almost all applications can set a standard hard, non-breaking space in place of the regular blank space, and some, like Adobe PageMaker, can set em, en, and thin spaces (see the charts in Appendix C). Use these blank spaces to indent lines of type so you have a strong flush alignment. If the space you set is too large, select that blank space and reduce the size of it.

"I knew who I was when
I woke up this morning,
but I must have changed
several times since then,"
said Alice.

"I knew who I was when
I woke up this morning,
but I must have changed
several times since then,"
said Alice.

In this example, I typed an en space in front of the first word of every line (except the first one) to align them with the first letter in the paragraph.

Reverse the punctuation

This next trick is kind of a kludge (which means a dorky solution), but it works: select the punctuation and paste it in front of (or at the end of, if flush right) each of the other lines. Select the punctuation you have pasted in and then choose the "reverse" style from your font formatting menu to make the characters invisible. (In a word processing application, you might not have the option to make type reverse.)

The reason I suggest you paste the punctuation instead of simply typing it is that very often when type is set fairly large (above 14 point), you need to reduce the size of the punctuation so it doesn't appear unnecessarily important. By pasting the punctuation, you ensure that all your reverse spaces are the same size, even if you changed the type sizes.

"To be successful,
sacrifices must be made.
It's better if they are
made by others
but failing that,
you'll have to
make them yourself."

Rita Mae Brown

A. *The punctuation needs to be hung.*

"To be successful,"
sacrifices must be made."
It's better if they are."
made by others."
but failing that,"
you'll have to."
make them yourself."

Rita Mae Brown."

B. *Paste in copies of the punctuation.*

"To be successful,
sacrifices must be made.
It's better if they are
made by others
but failing that,
you'll have to
make them yourself."

Rita Mae Brown

C. *Reverse the punctuation you don't need.*

Kern outside the text block or box

In PageMaker or QuarkXPress, try this: Type a hard space *in front of* the first quotation mark. Then kern until the quotation mark hangs outside the text block or box. The mark will seem to disappear, but in PageMaker, you will see the quotation mark as soon as you redraw your screen. In Quark-XPress, you won't ever see that quotation mark, but it will print just fine.

To do this with flush right text, follow these steps: *After* the last quotation mark, type a hard space. Then hit the left arrow key once so the insertion point moves to the left of the hard space. Now kern and the quotation mark and period will move outside the block or box.

To type this:	Mac	Windows
regular hard space	Option Spacebar	Alt 0160

"We haven't the money,
so we've got to think."

Lord Rutherford

Notice the quotation mark is hanging outside of the text block.

"We haven't the money,
so we've got to think."

Lord Rutherford

The quotation mark is hanging off the right edge, but since both lines have punctuation, the period does not need to hang outside also. I added a thin space after "Lord Rutherford" to visually align it with the text above.

Punctuation Style

All of us are now circumventing the professional typesetter and creating beautiful publications on our own desktops. We've heard all about the typesetting standards of setting one space after periods, and how to access em dashes and en dashes and true quotation marks and apostrophes. Although most of us know how to *create* these alternate characters, there still seems to be considerable confusion over *when* to use them. The punctuation in your publication affects the professional appearance of your work just as powerfully as the characters themselves. (It's interesting that when the "rules" of design are broken it is called "creative," but when the established rules of punctuation are broken it is called "uneducated." Creative punctuation isn't a well-accepted idea.)

So following are some guidelines to help give your desktop-designed work a more professional edge. If you have other questions, read *The Chicago Manual of Style,* William Strunk's wonderful little book, *The Elements of Style,* or check out the back of your dictionary—most dictionaries include a basic manual of style.

It is often the very small details that set mediocre work apart from outstanding work. To push a publication to the professional edge, make sure you carry your style all the way through, even to such mundane principles as punctuation.

Quotation Marks

Of course you are using proper quotation marks (" ") and not typewriter marks ("). American standards decree that periods and commas be placed inside quotation marks, *always.* Yes, I know, the logical thing to do is to place them inside or outside depending on whether the comma or period belongs to the material in the quotes or not. Like it or not, that's not the way it is in America; some other countries do it differently.

> "Oh Bear," said Christopher Robin, "How I do love you."
> "So do I," said Pooh.

Colons and **semicolons** are always placed *outside* the quotation marks, and they are both followed by one space.

> This is how to pronounce "forte": fort.
> Most people mispronounce "victuals"; it is properly
>   pronounced "vittles."

Exclamation points and **question marks** follow logic: If the mark belongs to the quoted matter, it goes inside. Otherwise it is set outside.

> She said, "I love to crack crawdads!"
> Did she say, "I love to crack crawdads"?
> She asked me, "Don't you love to crack crawdads?"
> My son warned me, "Mom, I met a girl who loves
>   to crack crawdads"!

Parentheses

If the text inside the parentheses is just an aside within or at the end of a sentence (like this one), then the punctuation goes after and *outside* the closing parenthesis.

If the text inside the parentheses is a complete sentence that starts with a capital letter and ends with a period (or other final mark), then the punctuation belongs *inside* the parentheses. (This is an example.)

There are no extra spaces surrounding parentheses, other than the normal word space before and after. There is no extra space between the closing parenthesis and any punctuation that might follow.

> **Meet me under the magnolia at twilight (without the wig), and we will waddle down the trail together.**
>
> *Notice the comma is directly after the parenthesis, and there is just the regular word space after the comma.*

Also see Chapter 7 for information on when you might need to shift the baseline position (up or down) of the parentheses.

Apostrophes

In contractions and informal writing, the apostrophe belongs where the letter is missing. Remember that simple principle and you will never go wrong. I repeat myself on this because it is so important, yet the misuse of the apostrophe is rampant and annoying.

In case you missed it: One of the two most common mistakes in typography is with the word **and** between words such as **Mom 'n' Pop** or **peaches 'n' cream.** Set the apostrophe where the letters are missing! If a letter or number is missing at the beginning of a word, *don't turn the apostrophe around so it looks like an opening single quote.* It *should* be an apostrophe.

To know where the apostrophe belongs in **possessive words,** turn the phrase around. The apostrophe belongs *after* the word in the turned phrase. For instance, "all the horses oats." Is it all the oats that belong to the *horse* (which would then be *horse's oats*) or all the oats that belong to the *horses* (which would then be *horses' oats*)? Notice the apostrophe is set after the word you used in the turned-around phrase.

Its or It's

The other most prevalent mistake in publications is in the word **its.** Do you put an apostrophe in the word *hers,* or *his,* or *theirs,* or *yours?* No, of course not. The word **its,** when possessive, is in the same category as hers, his, and yours—*there is no apostrophe!* **It's** with an apostrophe always, always, always, is a contraction for **it is** (or *it has*). **Always.**

Ellipsis

The ellipsis character (the three dots: . . .) is used to indicate where text has been omitted from the original material. There is a character on your keyboard for this (see below). But this character is too tight for professional typographic standards. You can type a space between periods, but then it might break at the end of a line and you would have one or two periods at the beginning of the next line. Preferably, type a thin or en space before and after each period (see the chart at the end of the book). If you can't type thin or en spaces, as in QuarkXPress, kern the three periods open. If you have an ellipsis at the end of a sentence, type a period after the ellipsis.

Wrong: **It's so...silly.**   Right: **It's so . . . silly.**

To type this:	Mac	Windows
ellipsis …	Option Semicolon	Alt 1033

Type style

The style of the punctuation should match the style of the word it follows. For instance, if a word followed by a comma is **bold,** then the comma itself should also be bold. You may have a semicolon following *italic words;* the semicolon should be italic. Follow the same principle for any style change.

Parentheses, though, do not pick up the style unless everything within the parentheses is the same style. That is, if all the text in the parentheses is italic, then the parentheses are both italic. But if only the last word is italic, the parentheses are set in the regular style of the rest of the text. The same goes for bold or any other style change. Like so:

She's willing (and able) and she'll be ready in a while.

She's willing (and I do believe she's ***able***), but not ready.

She's willing *(but not able)* and will be ready in a while.

Don't worry if you at first think it looks a little odd to have a big fat bold period or comma in the middle of your **paragraph,** like so. This is one of those things you get used to and then the wrong way soon begins to look glaringly wrong. It's like knowing that the pronunciation of the word **forte** (as in "Pickle-making is my forte") is really "fort," not "fortay." The word "fortay" means "loud, forcefully," as in music notation. At first it sounds wrong to say "fort," and you must have conviction to pronounce it properly among others who assume you are wrong, since most people pronounce it incorrectly. But once you accept that "fort" is the correct pronunciation, "fortay" is wrong (unless you choose to use a dictionary that has succumbed to popular pronunciation rather than correctness, which is what happens to our language anyway). (Oh well.)

Em dashes

Text within parentheses is like whispering; text within commas is an average statement; text within em dashes is more emphatic. The example below illustrates this concept.

Use em dashes to set off a phrase that has a lot of commas in it—like this, and thus, and so—to avoid confusing the reader.

Or mark an abrupt change in thought or sentence structure—how does this look—with an em dash.

Em dashes are set with no space before or after the dash. This bothers many people, though, because the dash tends to bump into the letters. So add a tiny bit of space on either side by kerning (see Chapter 14 on Kerning). But if you insert an entire word space before and after the dash, you exacerbate the interruption in the flow of text.

The origins of printing are almost as obscure as the origins of writing, and for much the same reason — its inventors never used their new medium to record the process.
Sean Morrison

When there is a space on either side of an em dash, it creates a disturbing gap in the text and calls too much attention to itself. Typeface is Memphis Light.

The origins of printing are almost as obscure as the origins of writing, and for much the same reason—its inventors never used their new medium to record the process.
Sean Morrison

Kern a little bit of space on either side of the em dash, if necessary, just enough so it doesn't bump into the letters.

To type this:	Mac	Windows
em dash —	Option Shift Hyphen	Alt 0151

En dashes

The most common use of an en dash is to indicate a duration. Read the sentence; if you substitute the word "to" for the dash, then the proper mark is an en dash. Actually, in a real sentence I would spell out the word "to," but you will often find occasions outside of sentences where an en dash is the appropriate mark.

> **All children ages 3–10 are welcome to attend**
> **the crawdad party from 6–8 P.M. every Monday**
> **from September–November.**

En dashes are commonly used with a little extra space on either side, especially when indicating a duration. Either add a little space with your kerning function, or insert a thin space on either side—*do not* type a whole word space with the Spacebar on either end of the en dash.

Also use an en dash instead of a hyphen in a compound adjective when one of the items is two words or a hyphenated word.

> **She took the New York–London plane to be at the opening**
> **of the post–Vietnam War presentation.**

> **The Internet cafe was filled with the over–sixty-five crowd.**

To type this:	Mac	Windows
en dash –	Option Hyphen	Alt 0150

Hyphens

Just because you know how to use em and en dashes, don't ignore hyphens! Em and en dashes do not replace hyphens—they simply replace *the incorrect uses of the hyphen.* If you are breaking a word at the end of a line (as in the line above), or if you are using a compound adjective as in "blue-green eyes," of course type a hyphen!

The following situation is difficult to describe, so I am going to illustrate it instead. When you have something like this:

> **Martha was both a first-place and second-place winner in the gravedigging contest.**

"First-place" and "second-place" are adjectives composed of two words, making them "compound." You probably want to combine those compound adjectives into something like this:

> **Martha was both a first- and second-place winner in the gravedigging contest.**

Does it bug you that the word "first" has a hyphen after it? Well, too bad because that is the correct way to set the text. The hyphen indicates that this word is also connected with the rest of the adjective. Once you understand and accept the correctness of it, you can have a little uppity attitude when you see others set it wrong. Gently teach them.

When to Shift that Baseline

Ahhh, so you have surely by now read *The Mac is not a typewriter* or *The PC is not a typewriter*, as well as the previous chapters in this book, and you have been diligently typing one space after periods, using real apostrophes and quotation marks, putting the apostrophes in the right places, and creating true fractions. Right? Now that you're feeling sassy, it's time to move on to a more sophisticated matter: baseline shift.*

First, let's clarify the term **baseline.** The baseline is the invisible line upon which all the characters sit, as shown below. Some characters, such as j, p, g, and y, have strokes that hang below the baseline; these strokes are called the "descenders." The term "baseline shift" refers to moving characters up or down in relation to that baseline.

I have a frog in my pocket, darling.

The grey line indicates the baseline of the text. Most characters are designed to sit directly on the baseline; descenders hang below.

Once you are familiar with the baseline shift technique, you will find uses for it more often than you might think!

---

* *The techniques in this chapter can only be accomplished in page layout programs, such as Adobe PageMaker or QuarkXPress. It's possible to do them in some word processing programs, but it takes much more effort. Check your manual.*

Parentheses and hyphens

I'll bet it drives you nuts that the hyphens in phone numbers seem set too low. And the parentheses around the area codes bump into the numbers, which probably makes you crazy. You see, parentheses and hyphens are designed to be used with lowercase letters, because that is where they appear most of the time. So when these characters are used with all caps or numbers, they appear to be low in relation to the taller size of the caps or numbers. But, thank goodness, this can be fixed.

Below, I shifted the hyphen and the parentheses up a little higher until they appeared to be centered—doesn't it look much better, more consistent, in better balance? There is no scientific formula for the exact placement—*your eye is the judge.* If it looks centered, it is. If it looks too low, it is. If it looks too high, it is.

(707) 123-4567

The parentheses bump into the tops of the numbers, but hang below the bottoms. Also notice how low the hyphen appears.

(707) 123-4567

To make parentheses and hyphens appear to be in the correct position when you're working with caps or numbers, raise them up a little.

The Cul-de-Sac reopens (dinner only)

THE CUL-DE-SAC REOPENS (DINNER ONLY)

THE CUL-DE-SAC REOPENS (DINNER ONLY)

Parentheses and hyphens are designed for lowercase letters, since that is where they are used most often (as in the first line). If you use all caps (second line), the hyphens and parentheses are too low. Raise them higher off the baseline to make them appear centered (third line).

Dingbats as bullets

Another occasion to take advantage of the baseline shift feature is when using dingbats or ornaments. Suppose you have a list of items and you really want to use a fancy dingbat from the Zapf Dingbats or Wingdings font, instead of using the boring ol' round bullet (or—heaven forbid—a hyphen). But the dingbat character is usually too big. When you reduce its size, though, the dingbat is too low because the character is still sitting on the baseline. So select the character and shift it up above the baseline.

Pick any three adjectives that describe yourself:
- lovely
- surly
- ghastly
- womanly
- manly
- saintly
- ungodly
- stately
- sprightly

A. *Choose a dingbat instead of the dumb ol' bullet*

Pick any three adjectives that describe yourself:
- ▼ lovely
- ❧ surly
- ✿ ghastly
- ☙ womanly
- ✈ manly
- ✣ saintly
- ♠ ungodly
- ■ stately
- ❖ sprightly

B. *You have lots of dingbats to choose from, but they are usually too big. (Choose one dingbat.)*

Pick any three adjectives that describe yourself:
- ▾ lovely
- ▾ surly
- ▾ ghastly
- ▾ womanly
- ▾ manly
- ▾ saintly
- ▾ ungodly
- ▾ stately
- ▾ sprightly

C. *You can decrease the point size of the bullet, but then it sits too low.*

Pick any three adjectives that describe yourself:
- ▾ lovely
- ▾ surly
- ▾ ghastly
- ▾ womanly
- ▾ manly
- ▾ saintly
- ▾ ungodly
- ▾ stately
- ▾ sprightly

D. *Raise the small dingbat higher off the baseline.*

Initial caps

You can also create a quick initial cap with baseline shift. Change the size and font and perhaps color of the first letter. If it disrupts the line spacing, select the entire paragraph and apply a fixed amount of leading (just type in a number—don't use "auto"; see Chapter 15). Then select the first letter and apply the baseline shift downward—making sure the baseline of the letter aligns on one of the baselines of the paragraph! (See Chapter 24 for lots of suggestions for initial caps.)

The important thing about your lot in life is whether you use it for building or parking.

In this paragraph, I selected the "T" and changed its typeface and size. I used the technique in Chapter 5 (hard space and kerning) to hang the "T" so it aligned with the rest of the text. I used the baseline shift feature to drop the bottom of the "T" down to the second line. I had to kern the "h" in toward the "T."

Typeface is Bernhard Modern.

Decorative words

You can also create interesting special effects with words, as shown below. Some of the letters have been shifted up, then kerned into the caps. The "D" has been shifted down slightly. The word "The" has been shifted up and kerned close, also.

The Sea Dollar

This arrangement was created with baseline shifts and kerning.

Typeface is ExPonto Multiple Master.

Corrections

Sometimes, especially in decorative type or logos, the characters are not exactly where you want them. So use your baseline shift to adjust their positions. Remember one of the Rules of Life: you are never stuck with anything. Get busy. Get creative.

This is the way the text set as I simply typed it. I wanted the apostrophe lower, and the Z to come down a bit to balance the word.

Typefaces are Las Bonitas Bold and Schablone Rough.

That's better, and that was easy.

Two paragraphs on one line

Have you ever wanted to create a format such as the one below and be able to apply it using style sheets for both the headings and the body copy? If you use style sheets, you know this is impossible because a style applies to the entire paragraph. (If you don't know how to use your style sheets, skip the rest as it will probably just confuse you.)

To create the effect shown below, do this: in the Heading style sheet, set the baseline shift to drop down to the first baseline of the body copy. Reduce the leading value of the Headings to reduce the amount of space above the paragraphs. Set an indent in the Body Copy style sheet.

Pronouns	What is the name of that surly bloke? I'm dying to meet him.
Prepositions	There wasn't a single item in my closet that I could don with impunity, nor was there a shoe fit to boogie in.
Conjunctions	The robot and the dentist tangoed beneath the stars.

Text from *The Deluxe Transitive Vampire* by Karen Elizabeth Gordon (the ultimate handbook of grammar)

I set an indent in the style sheet for the Body Copy. I set a very small leading amount in the Heading style sheet, then I played with baseline shift until the baseline of the Heading landed directly on the baseline of the next paragraph, the indented Body Copy.

How do you do it?

To baseline shift, first select the character(s). Then:

- **In Adobe PageMaker,** use the Control Palette: type in a positive or negative amount in the bottom right corner, or click the tiny nudge arrows up or down. To nudge in an amount that is ten times the increment you have set in your Preferences dialog box, hold down the Shift key (in Mac versions before 6.5, use the Command key) .

  Or use the Type Specs dialog box; click on "Options...."

  You can add baseline shift to your style sheet.

- **In Mac QuarkXPress,** select the text, then:
to move up	Command Option Shift +
to move down	Command Option Shift -

  (Use the + and - from the keyboard, not the numeric keypad).

  In Windows QuarkXPress, select the text, then:
to move up	Control Alt Shift)
to move down	Control Alt Shift (

- *Or* **in either Mac or Windows:**

  From the Style menu, choose "Baseline Shift" or "Character" and type in a number in the "Baseline Shift" area in that dialog box.

  You can add baseline shift to your style sheet.

Expert Type

In which we look at
true-drawn small caps,
compressed and
expanded characters,
as well as ligatures and
oldstyle figures (numbers).

We also explore
expert sets and
discuss display type.

That is a beautiful occupation.
And since it is beautiful, it is truly useful.

The Little Prince, Antoine de Saint-Exupery

Expert Sets

What I love most about the revolution in electronic design and communi-cation is the explosion in the awareness of typography. People who, ten years ago, didn't know there was more than one typeface in the world now scrutinize menus and advertisements and posters, wondering what font is on the page. It also never ceases to amaze me how quickly we become inured to the magic, how quickly we find that what we have isn't enough and we want more and better and bigger. It's hard to imagine that we could want more than the standard set of 256 characters in a typical font, which is many more than we had on our typewriters. But we do, and that's just the way it is. And that's why several of the major font vendors created **expert sets,** additions to basic font sets that are designed for when we get to that point of wanting more and better.

What's in an expert set?

This chapter is an introduction to the concept of expert sets. The following chapters in this section elaborate on the various typographic features, such as those listed below, that you'll find in these special fonts.

Small Caps

Almost any program can turn selected lowercase letters into SMALL CAPS, where a capital is still a capital and the other letters become capital letters about the height of lowercase letters. The problem, though, is that the computer simply reduces the size of the existing capital letters. This creates a proportion distortion between the cap and the small cap, where the capital letter appears much heavier than the corresponding smaller capitals. In expert sets, the small caps are not just small capitals, but are letterforms that have been totally redesigned to visually match the large cap in the same point size. See Chapter 9.

Oldstyle figures

Regular numbers (figures), such as 45,872, appear too large when set within body text. Numbers used to be designed like lowercase letters, with ascenders and descenders, like so: 45,872. Expert sets include these oldstyle figures, which blend smoothly with the body copy. Oldstyle figures are also particularly beautiful when set in extra-large sizes. Once you start using them it's hard to go back to the other numbers. See Chapter 10.

Display type or titling caps

Traditionally, small letterforms and large letterforms in a well-designed typeface differ not just in their height, but in their thick/thin stroke differences, the proportion of the x-height to the cap height of the character, the space between the letters, and the open space in the "counters" (the holes in letters like e, g, or c). But on the computer when you use a large point size of a regular font, say 127 point, the computer just takes the 12 point size and enlarges it to 127 point. The letterforms start looking a little clunky.

Several of the expert font sets offer display type (which includes lowercase) or titling capitals. The characters in display typefaces have been specially designed for larger sizes, those above 24 point. The difference isn't readily noticeable at 24 point, but becomes quite significant on headline or poster-sized type. See Chapter 13.

Ligatures

In addition to the standard ligatures *fi* and *fl* (Mac only) expert sets usually offer a few more combinations (even an Rp for rupees). See Chapter 11.

Swash characters

The more elaborate expert sets offer alternate swash characters that can add a very nice touch to your work. *R*emember, swash characters are like cheesecake—it's easy to overdose. And be sensible where you place them. The swash is meant to end a phrase or tuck under adjacent letters, not to create an unsightly gap. *See Chapter 23.*

Em dashes

Convention decrees that we set em dashes with no space on either side— like so. But those long dashes often bump right into the letters and have to be manually letterfit. Many people insist on using a space on either side of the em dash, which exacerbates the interruption in the reading and creates an even larger gap in the overall look of the type. Some expert sets contain a wonderful character that solves this problem—a ¾-em dash with a thin space built into both sides. You have to look for it, unfortunately.

Ornaments

There are often pretty little ornaments (❧ — ❧ ❧ ～ ❧ ⸺) in the expert sets that offer elegant alternatives to dingbats. See Chapter 26.

Realities of using expert sets

The deterrent to using expert sets in everyday work is that they are actually different fonts that contain only the special characters. If you type an address, for instance, you have to switch from your regular font to the expert font for the numbers, then back to the regular font again. To use the 3/4-em dash you must change fonts for that one character. Every time you add a swash character you must change fonts. In many expert sets, the small caps font has no large caps at all, so every word that contains a regular cap in addition to small caps requires two font changes. To simplify matters you can often use search-and-replace. Or you might want to set up a macro or quick-key for switching. For this book I have used the Caslon expert set, and I use WYSIWYG Menus from Now Utilities on my Mac not only because it keeps my font menu manageable, but because it also allows me to set hot keys—I can type a key to change fonts. This makes using an expert set so much more pleasant.

Another problem with the expert sets is that the vendors don't always provide much information on the characters that are available, where they might be useful, what some of those strange symbols are good for, or how to access all of them. Some of the sets have hidden characters that are difficult to discover, such as those that take four keys to produce (such as: Option Y, then Shift N).

Font utilities

To find and use the special characters, you'll need an extra little font utility. If you're on a Mac, go to **www.shareware.com** and download either the free version or the inexpensive shareware version of PopChar, read the directions, and use it. When you buy an Adobe expert set for the Mac, it comes with a special utility called KeyCap which gives you a chart of the special characters. If you're on a PC, use the Character Map that you find in your Start menu. See Appendix C for more details. Mac users, you might want to take a look at my book, *How to Boss Your Fonts Around, Second Edition.*

If you are adept at working with a large number of fonts, then you probably already use a font management utility like Font Reserve, Suitcase, Adobe Type Manager Deluxe, or MasterJuggler on the Mac, or Adobe Type Manager Deluxe on a Windows machine. It's practically a requirement to use one of these utilities (and a font menu utility) with the larger expert font collections, like Adobe's Minion (22 fonts) or Linotype's Centennial (17 fonts). The Caslon face I am using for this book totals 26 separate fonts.

These families include such treats as more weights, swashes, display type, titling caps, caption fonts, super- and subscript numbers in proportion to the typeface, and/or ornaments.

The subtle distinctions the expert sets offer would have passed fairly unnoticed in the general public years ago. But the level of type sophistication has increased so dramatically across an incredible variety of professions, so the subtle distinctions in type are now being noticed and appreciated. Even though the changes are what some may call minor, the overall professional effect comes through clearly.

As we drive up the river road, there are sixty thousand trees I see but do not touch. Like me, Amanda is confined in the speeding jeep, but she touches every tree.

notebook of Marx Marvelous
another roadside attraction,
by Tom Robbins

This is just a simple example of the difference the specialty fonts in an expert set can make in a piece of type. To the left is plain ol' Times Roman, 12/14.5.

*A*S WE DRIVE UP THE RIVER ROAD, there are sixty thousand trees I see but do not touch. Like me, *A*manda is confined in the speeding jeep, but she touches every tree.

~ *notebook of Marx Marvelous*
   ANOTHER ROADSIDE ATTRACTION,
   by Tom Robbins

This is Minion Regular, 11/16, with expert small caps, display swash italic, regular swash italic, and an ornament.

✓Caslon ▶	Bold
City names ▶	*Bold Italic*
Clarendon ▶	*Italic* ☐F11
Display ▶	✓ Regular ☐F12
Eurostile ▶	Semibold
ExPonto ▶	*Semibold Italic*
Flyer ▶	Alt Bold
Formata ▶	Alt Bold Italic
Garamond ▶	Alt Italic
JimboMM ▶	Alt Regular
LW ROM ▶	Alt Semibold
Memphis ▶	Alt Semibold Italic
Minion ▶	Big Alternates
MottocorMM ▶	BIG EXPERT
Onyx	Big Roman
Optima ▶	BIG SMALL CAPS
Script ▶	expert bold
Toulouse ▶	expert Bold Italic
Trade Gothic ▶	expert Italic
Veljovic ▶	EXPERT REGULAR ☐F10
Zapf Renaissance ▶	EXPERT SEMIBOLD
	expert Semibold Italic
	✿❀❁❃❋❄✿❄
	Swash Bold Italic
	Swash Italic
	Swash Semibold Italic

This is my font menu for Caslon, the typeface you are reading in this book. Each of these names is a separate font.

I used **WYSIWYG Menus** *from Now Utilities to group my fonts into families. This is only available for the Macintosh.*

Notice the hot keys listed to the right of several fonts—using Now Menus, I can just hit that key and the next character I type will be in that font, or the selected text will turn into that font. This feature is so valuable when doing a lot of work with expert sets.

You also need something like the freeware utility **PopChar** *that lets you view all the characters in the set and insert them without having to know the key combinations.*

✓ A Caslon-Italic ▶	Alt Regular
A Caslon Expert ▶	Ornaments
Antique Olive-Roman ▶	Regular
EmmascriptMUB	Alt Italic
Eurostile Condensed ▶	✓ Italic
Zapf Dingbats	Swash Italic
	Alt Semi Bold
All ▶	Alt Semi Bold Italic
Font Book ▶	Swash Semi Bold Italic
	Alt Bold
TypeTamer®	Bold
	Alt Bold Italic
	Bold Italic
	Swash Bold Italic

Or instead of those two separate utilities mentioned above, you can use a great utility called **TypeTamer** *from Impossible Software (except you won't have hot keys). You can see the face and find the special characters right from the menu. Again, this is only available for the Macintosh.*

A Caslon-Bold Italic Type: PostScript

IT'S VERY SIMPLE—either you run or you get busy.

Position your pointer over the icon in the menu and you will see a display of the typeface (you can change the size and the text of the display). Hold down the Option key or Command Option and you'll see all the special characters available. Choose the special character you want and it appears on your page wherever the insertion point was flashing.

Actually, what I generally use is **Adobe Type Reunion Deluxe,** *which lets me group fonts into categories. It does not have hot keys, though, nor does it show the special characters. Available for the Macintosh only.*

Small Caps

THERE ARE A NUMBER OF TECHNIQUES that designers and typographers use to make type more beautiful and pleasant—one technique is the use of small caps. Small caps are capital letters that are approximately the size of lowercase letters. Small caps are often used simply for their design effect, but they have several very practical uses in fine typography. Sometimes an article or chapter opening begins with the first line (or part of the first line) in small caps, as in this paragraph. This is a simple and elegant way to lead the reader into the text.

Where to use small caps

If you set acronyms in regular all caps, their visual presence is unnecessarily overwhelming. One standard and practical place to use small caps is in acronyms such as FBI, NRC, CBS, or SIMM.

Traditionally, "A.M." and "P.M." are set with small caps. If you were taught to type on a typewriter (or if you were taught on a keyboard by someone who was taught on a typewriter), you probably learned to set these abbreviations in all caps because there were no small caps on typewriters. But now that you have the capability, you can and should set them properly.

Harriet, an FBI agent, turned on CNN to get the dirt
on the CIA before going to bed at 9:30 P.M.

Harriet, an FBI agent, turned on CNN to get the dirt
on the CIA before going to bed at 9:30 P.M.

*The capital letters in the middle of the sentence call too much attention
to themselves. Notice how the small caps blend in with the text.
The capital letters for P.M. are much too large—
the abbreviation is not that important.*

Creating small caps on your computer

Most programs have a command in the Format or Font menu to change selected lowercase letters to small caps. If not, type the text in all caps and then reduce the selected letters to about 70 percent of the point size of the rest of the type (this is what the computer shortcut does).

These two methods are okay if you are going to use small caps just once in a while on fairly low-level jobs. But if you are producing fine typography, you really need to invest in a typeface that has specially designed small caps. When you simply reduce the point size of the type (the same thing the computer does when you use a menu command), all the proportions are reduced and the thickness of the strokes of the smaller letters no longer matches the thickness of the regular caps in the same sentence.

THERE IS NO REST FOR THE WICKED.

*The weight of the computer-drawn small caps
is thinner than the weight of the regular initial (first letter) caps.
Typeface is Eurostile Condensed.*

If you need to use a face that does not have a matching set for small caps, try using the semibold face (if there is one) for the small caps, since when you reduce their size their line thickness will shrink. Or you can try changing the default size of the small caps—if your application sets small caps at 70 percent, try changing that to 82 percent to match the stroke thickness better. Unfortunately, in QuarkXPress the small cap size applies to your entire document—to every font, every size, every style, every weight. This is very poor typographic handling. In PageMaker you can change the small cap size per character, and you can add it to your style sheets.

True-drawn small caps

There are quite a few font families that include "true-drawn" small caps. True-drawn small caps are letterforms that have been totally redesigned as small caps specifically to match the proportions and thicknesses of the matching uppercase. These families are often called "expert" sets or perhaps "small cap" sets (see Chapter 8). The result creates an undisturbing, smooth, uniform, tone throughout the text.

THERE IS NO REST
FOR THE WICKED.

THE WICKED ARE VERY WEARY.

*True-drawn small caps are specially drawn
to match the weight of the capital letters in the same face.*

*Typefaces are Caslon Semibold, Caslon Expert Semibold,
Caslon Regular, Caslon Expert Regular.*

Readability and legibility of small caps

Pull quotes and captions are sometimes set with small caps, but keep in mind that small caps are no easier to read than all caps. Since every word in all caps is a rectangle, our eyes have to resort to reading letter by letter. This does not mean you should *never* use all caps or small caps—just be aware of this limitation and use them when you can justify the loss in readability and legibility. The more text there is in all caps or small caps, the less likely it is that people will read it.

TO LIVE CONTENT WITH SMALL MEANS; TO SEEK ELEGANCE RATHER THAN LUXURY, AND REFINEMENT RATHER THAN FASHION; TO BE WORTHY, NOT RESPECTABLE, AND WEALTHY, NOT RICH; TO STUDY HARD, THINK QUIETLY, TALK GENTLY, AND ACT FRANKLY; TO LISTEN TO STARS AND BIRDS, TO BABES AND SAGES, WITH OPEN HEART; TO BEAR ALL CHEERFULLY, DO ALL BRAVELY, AWAIT OCCASIONS, HURRY NEVER. IN A WORD, TO LET THE SPIRITUAL, UNBIDDEN AND UNCONSCIOUS, GROW UP THROUGH THE COMMON. THIS IS TO BE MY SYMPHONY.
WILLIAM HENRY CHANNING

Do you find that, even though the text is interesting, you have to struggle to stay with it? Small caps are no easier to read than all caps.

Oldstyle Figures

In typography, numbers are called figures. Most typefaces use plain old regular numbers, or figures. These regular numbers (also called "lining figures") are similar to all caps in that they appear to be too large when set within body text. But figures used to be designed like lowercase letters, with ascenders and descenders, which blend smoothly and beautifully with body copy. These "oldstyle figures" are also particularly beautiful when set in large sizes. Once you start using them it's hard to go back to the regular lining number.

Notice how large and clunky these numbers appear:

Dear John, please call me at 438-9762 at 3:00 to discuss marriage.
Or write to me at Route 916, zip code 87505.

Notice how beautifully these numbers blend into the text:

Dear John, please call me at 438-9762 at 3:00 to discuss marriage.
Or write to me at Route 916, zip code 87505.

Monospaced figures

Regular, or lining, figures are not proportionally spaced as letters are; they are monospaced. That is, every regular number takes up the same amount of space: the number one occupies as much space as the number seven. This is necessary because we often need to make columns of numbers and the numbers need to align in the columns.

Rats	**473**	*If the numbers were not monospaced,*
Ravens	**1,892**	*we would have great difficulty*
Robots	**19.5**	*aligning them in columns.*

But when you use regular, lining figures in body text, the monospacing creates awkward letter spacing and usually requires kerning. Look carefully at the letter spacing in the numbers below:

Call Rosalind at 1.916.987.7546.

Proportionally spaced figures

In most (not all) expert fonts, the oldstyle figures are proportionally spaced, meaning they each take up only as much space as is appropriate for the number—the number one takes up less space than a nine because it's skinnier. This is particularly wonderful for text use because the numbers fit together so well, but don't use proportionally spaced oldstyle figures in columns to be summed or they won't line up! When you buy an expert set and start using oldstyle figures, first make a quick check to see if yours are proportionally spaced or monospaced: just type several rows in columns and see if you can draw a clean line between each column.

1234567	1234567	*Because the numbers on the left are monospaced, they align neatly in columns. The numbers on the right are proportionally spaced, so they do not align in columns.*
4598021	4598021	
9768635	9768635	

Ligatures

Ligatures are single typographic characters that are combinations of two or more characters. For instance, there are common ligatures for the "fi" and "fl" combination:

fickle flames   fickle flames

Can you see the problems in the example on the left?
Can you see the solutions in the example on the right?

Ligatures are created either to solve a typographic problem, such as the hook of an "f" bumping into the dot of an "i," or sometimes simply for an elegant look. Almost every Macintosh font contains at least the fi and fl ligature, but you will find quite a range of ligatures in expert sets. Fonts for Windows machines do not contain even the fi and fl ligature—if you want to use them, you will have to buy a special expert set.

How many ligatures can you find in the following paragraph?

However, a good laugh is a mighty good thing, and rather too scarce a good thing; the more's the pity. So, if any one man, in his own proper person, afford stuff for a good joke to anybody, let him not be backward, but let him cheerfully allow himself to spend and to be spent in that way, and the man that has anything bountifully laughable about him, be sure there is more in that man than you perhaps think for.

Herman Melville, Moby Dick

These are the ligatures available in the font Zapf Renaissance Italic Swash, which is designed to be set with the font Zapf Renaissance Italic, (both of which are shown to the left):

ff sp fi stff th Th fl fl ffl ffi f

Setting ligatures

You can always set the fi and fl ligatures in just about any font on the Macintosh. If you want other ligatures, or if you use a PC, you will have to invest in an expert font set.

fi   Option Shift 5

fl   Option Shift 6

In Mac QuarkXPress, there is a feature that automatically sets the ligatures whenever you type "fi" or "fl" in the document. From the Edit menu, slide down to "Preferences," out to "Document," and click the "Character" tab. (In version 3.3, choose "Typographic" from the "Preferences" submenu.) Check the "Ligatures" checkbox. The "Break Above" amount is a kerning value so if you letterspace your type beyond that amount, the ligature will automatically separate back into the two separate characters.

The dotless i

Generally, ligatures are not used in display type (type in large sizes, above 24-point). If you have a problem with the hook of the "f" bumping into the dot of the "i," try using the dotless i character: ı (type Option Shift B). Again, this character is only available in Macintosh fonts.

Flying fish found in pocket!

Notice the problem in the "fi" combination.

Flying fish found in pocket!

The dotless i solves this problem so neatly.

This dotless i character also comes in handy any other time the dot gets in the way, as might happen if you use italic swash caps.

Victor Hugo   Victor Hugo

Oooh, doesn't that dot bumping into the V bother you? Now you can fix it.

Condensed and Extended Type

Type families often have more members than the basic Regular, Italic, Bold, and Bold Italic. A larger family might have Condensed, Bold Condensed, Extra Condensed, Extended, Black Extended, etc. Other typefaces are single-member families and are designed specifically as one very condensed or very extended look.

Condensed type is type that looks like it has been *compressed,* or squished, horizontally, but not vertically. **Extended** type seems to have been *expanded,* or stretched horizontally. You can use condensed or extended type for practical typographic solutions or simply for playful effects.

This is Eurostile Plain, a great face.

This is Eurostile Condensed, another great face.

This is Eurostile Extended, also great.

Condensed faces often have a "tall," elegant look. Extended faces usually appear squatty, yet appealing. They often have a high-tech, assertive look.

Condensed text faces

Condensed text faces are handy when space is at a premium. You've probably noticed that some typefaces take up a lot more room than others. Compare the space occupied by the copy set in the two faces below, Garamond and Times. Times was created for the *London Times* specifically to save space yet still be eminently readable. You can tell even in this small sample that a large body of text in Times would fill significantly less space than the same size type in Garamond, even though Times appears to be larger (because of its x-height; see page 17 for details about the x-height).

They have a wonderful therapeutic effect upon me, these catastrophes which I proofread . . . . When the world blows up and the final edition has gone to press the proofreaders will quietly gather up all commas, semicolons, hyphens, asterisks, brackets, parentheses, periods, exclamation marks, etc. and put them in a little box over the editorial chair. *Comme ça tout est régle.*

Henry Miller, *Tropic of Cancer*

They have a wonderful therapeutic effect upon me, these catastrophes which I proofread . . . . When the world blows up and the final edition has gone to press the proofreaders will quietly gather up all commas, semicolons, hyphens, asterisks, brackets, parentheses, periods, exclamation marks, etc. and put them in a little box over the editorial chair. *Comme ça tout est régle.*

Henry Miller, *Tropic of Cancer*

The face on the left is Garamond; on the right is Times.

Computer-drawn vs. true-drawn

You probably know you can compress and expand type through most software applications with the click of a button. This is okay for an occasional emergency, but the computer distorts the type by simply squishing it. If you need a compressed face so you can, for instance, get more words into your newsletter, please don't let the computer squish the type—invest in a "true-drawn" condensed face. True-drawn faces have been redesigned with different proportions, stroke thicknesses, counter spaces, and other fine features so as to retain the integrity of the typeface and maintain readability. Below are examples of what the computer does to the letterforms as opposed to what the designer does.

Franklin Gothic, condensed
Franklin Gothic Condensed

In the first example, the computer simply squished the letterforms. The second example is a redesigned face. Notice the differences in the weight, the thin/thick strokes, the counters (spaces inside the letters), the letter spacing, the height of the lowercase letters in relation to the caps, the terminals of the "e" and "s" where open space has been designed into the condensed version, and other subtle differences between the computerized version and the redesigned face.

As for me, I am tormented
with an everlasting itch
for things remote.
I love to sail forbidden seas
and land on barbarous coasts.

Herman Melville, *Moby Dick*

A well-designed condensed text face maintains maximum readability within the compressed proportions. This is an example of a true-drawn Garamond text face called Garamond Light Condensed.

Break the rules

Occasionally you may want to create some dynamic display of type and you need a condensed or extended version, but it doesn't exist or it isn't enough. It's okay to break the rules, but break them with gusto! Make it look like you *meant* to distort the type. If it's not obvious, the sophisticated reader (of which there are more and more) will think you just didn't know what you were doing. Don't be a wimp!

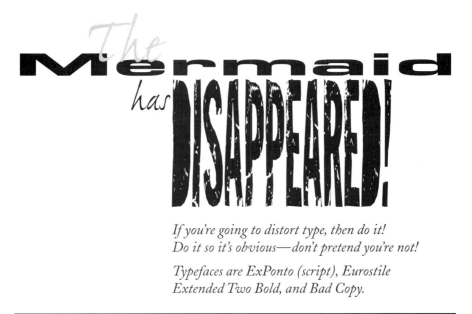

If you're going to distort type, then do it!
Do it so it's obvious—don't pretend you're not!

Typefaces are ExPonto (script), Eurostile
Extended Two Bold, and Bad Copy.

Display Type

Display type refers to type that is large, that is on display, as opposed to body text, which is what you read in paragraphs at smaller point sizes (9 to 12 point). Some people might refer to headlines as display type, but generally it refers to type around 24 points or above. Decorative typefaces are also called display faces, because you would typically use them only at large sizes for special occasions.

Now, the definitions above are generic definitions. There is also an actual classification of type design called "display type." These faces have been specifically redesigned for larger sizes.

Long ago, when type was carved by hand out of metal, the designer changed subtle features as the sizes got larger: the thin strokes got thinner, the serifs were more delicate, the counters (the space inside the letters) were different, the places where parts of the letters joined were thinner, the letter spacing was tighter, sometimes the ratio of x-height to cap height was different.

The computer, however, makes no distinction between sizes of type. It takes one size, say 12 point, and makes it larger or smaller as you wish. Thus when you use 6-point type, it is simply half of 12-point. This means the strokes are half as heavy, the space between the characters is half as much, etc. When you set 36-point type, it is simply three times as large as 12—the thin strokes are three times thicker, there is more space between the characters, etc. This creates a heavy, clunky look at large sizes. The solution to this problem is to use a specially designed display face.

Display vs. text

It is easy to see the differences in the two faces below. Both are the typeface Minion, but the word on the left is set with Minion Regular; the word on the right is set with Minion Display Regular. The instant impression, even if a person is typographically illiterate, is that the display face is finer and more elegant, less chunky and clunky. That's because the letterforms and spacing attributes in the display face have been designed specifically for larger type sizes—they have not been simply enlarged.

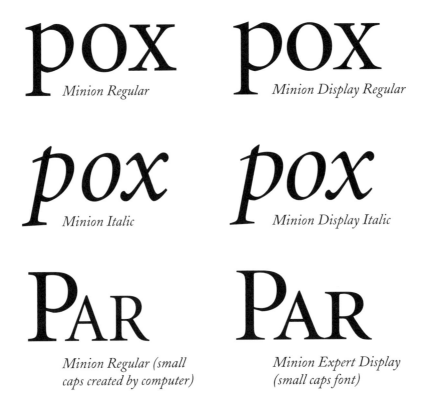

Minion Regular

Minion Display Regular

Minion Italic

Minion Display Italic

Minion Regular (small caps created by computer)

Minion Expert Display (small caps font)

Take notice of exactly what makes these faces different, which details create the more elegant look of the display face. Look carefully at the serifs, the thick/thin contrasts in the strokes, the places where the parts of the characters join together, the letter spacing, the crispness of the terminals. Which would you choose to use in a billboard or large poster?

Display type and body text

If you have a display face, don't use it in body text! If the computer takes a display face and reduces it, those delicate thins and serifs will be so weak in the smaller size that they'll fall apart when it prints. Remember, if the face was designed at 36-point and you print it at 9, the computer will just reduce everything in the entire face to a quarter of the original. Even if it prints well because you use a high-quality press, it will be less readable than the regular font at the smaller size.

Below is Caslon Regular from Adobe Systems set at 65–point. It's not really meant for large sizes.

Serendipity

But Caslon Regular *is* meant for body text. It holds up quite well at this size you are reading right now. Even at 9-point, the strokes are even and full, and the proportions are ideally suited for readable text.

Below is Big Caslon, a display face designed by Matthew Carter, set at 65-point. Although the features of this typeface are more delicately designed than the regular Caslon face, the Big Caslon presents a stronger presence on the page at the larger size.

Serendipity

But Big Caslon, the display face, is not readable or graceful at this small size you are reading right now. The proportion of the x-height is too large, the thins are too thin, the letter spacing is too tight, the delicate features are lost or wimpy.

yOU cAN dO A gOOD aD wITHOUT gOOd tYPOGrAPHY,
bUT yOU cAN'T dO A gREAT aD wITHOUT goOD tYPOGRAPHY.

hERB LuBALIN

Spacing

In which we discuss
the importance of
and uses for
pair kerning,
auto kerning,
range kerning,
track kerning,
manual kerning,
word spacing,
and letter spacing,
as well as
linespacing (leading)
and paragraph spacing.

The truth is

that typography is an ART
in which Violent Revolutions can scarcely,
in the nature of things,
hope to be successful.
A type of Revolutionary Novelty
may be extremely beautiful in itself;
but for the creatures of habit that we are,
its very Novelty
tends to make it illegiblE.

Aldous Huxley
Typography for the Twentieth-Century Reader

Kerning

In page layout applications, such as Adobe PageMaker, QuarkXPress, or Adobe FrameMaker, you have an incredible amount of control over the spacing between letters, words, and lines. But to take advantage of this control, you must know what the features refer to. Later in this section I address the space between lines (linespacing, or leading) and the space between paragraphs. This chapter focuses on manipulating the space between the letters: kerning, pair kerning, auto kerning, manual kerning, range kerning, tracking, and letter spacing.

Kerning

Kerning is the process of adjusting the space between individual letters; it is a fine-tuning process. The desirable end result is visually consistent letter spacing because consistent spacing strengthens the readability of the text. Whether that means you increase space between tight letters or decrease space between loose letters, the spacing must be consistent. You don't want the reader's eye to stumble over awkward letterfitting. To a discerning eye, your kerning is symbolic of your attitude and experience toward type. Don't be a dork.

Canteloupe

This word is not kerned at all. The letters are loose, quite separate from each other.

Canteloupe

This word has been kerned so the letters fit snugly and consistently together without being overly tight.

Kerning metal type

Until the 1970s, type was set in metal. Some machines set entire lines of type on metal slugs, but many machines followed the older style of using individual pieces. Regardless of the particular method, every character had its own separate metal space. If each letter is on its own piece of lead, then the letters can only get so close to each other—it's simply not physically possible to move them closer without taking a knife and shearing off some of the lead, thereby making that character useless for further typesetting. In lines of metal type, you couldn't even do that much. In those days, designers had to cut apart the proof sheets of type and move the printed letters around to adjust their spacing, then glue them down. If you look at an old magazine, you can instantly tell it's old, right? One of the visual clues that tells you it's old is the loose letter spacing, looser than you are accustomed to reading now that type is being set electronically.

Letter spacing

Letter spacing is not really kerning, but refers to a general and arbitrary adjustment of the space between characters in a large piece of text, whereas kerning is a form of individual letter spacing. You might want to add more letter space to open the look of a typeface, or to create a dramatic headline that stretches across the page. You might want to decrease the letter spacing of a script face so the connectors reach the following letters. Notice the very open (too open) letter spacing of this paragraph. It's rather annoying in this case, isn't it?

Whew. This is better. PageMaker's letter spacing values are based on the value the designer built into the font, and they are paragraph-specific so you can adjust the letter spacing appropriately according to the typeface and size and purpose. In QuarkXPress all you can do is change the "tracking" value, which merely adds or subtracts an arbitrary amount between all characters.

Kerning pairs

Most fonts have "kerning pairs" built into them. That is, as designers create fonts, they build in tighter spacing between certain *pairs* of letters that are known to cause inconsistent gaps, such as Ta, To, Yo, we, and many others. Not all fonts have kerning pairs built in, and some have poorly adjusted pairs. Some fonts have 200–300 kerning pairs, others have over a thousand. Just because a font has an extraordinary number of kerning pairs does not mean it's better. In fact, when there are thousands of pairs it can take an interminable length of time to display the text on the screen, and it will also take longer to print.

Auto kerning

Page layout applications usually have a checkbox that allows you to tell your program to automatically take advantage of the kerning pairs, if you are using a font that contains them. In most programs you can usually also specify a point size above which the kerning pairs are automatically used. It's neither necessary nor desirable to auto kern small sizes of type (less than about 7 or 8 point) because when type is set small it should actually have *more* space between characters, not less.

Well Told Vermin Take woe
Well Told Vermin Take woe

In the first example, no auto pair kerns have been used. In the second example, the automatic kerning pairs have been used. You can clearly see the difference, although in type this large you must still do some manual kerning—auto pair kerning is just a start. Look carefully to find where some manual kerning is needed. How about between the capital "V" and the lowercase "e"? The auto kerning brought them closer, but to make the spacing consistent, the pair could still scoot together a wee bit more.

Manual kerning

Kerning is a totally visual skill. The computer does the best it can with what it has to work with, but the end result, especially for larger type sizes, depends entirely on your eyes and your judgment. So even if your application has used auto pair-kerning, you must usually kern the larger type manually, selecting the space between two letters and adjusting it to match the visual space between the others.

Every page layout application and many illustration programs have keyboard shortcuts for kerning type on the screen. Sometimes you must insert a numeric value into a dialog box to add or remove the space, and some applications use both methods. Whatever it is, find out and use it.

 *When you kern manually, you must either select the two letters you wish to kern between, or click to set the insertion point between the two (depending on your software).*

Range kerning

Sometimes you start the fine-tuning process by selecting a "range" of text—a group of consecutive letters—and applying kerning values. This method, called range kerning, applies the same amount of space between every pair of letters, regardless of their natural letterfit. If you range kern, you will probably need to finish the process by manually kerning certain combinations.

 *When you select a range of text (as shown to the left) and apply a kerning value or use keyboard shortcuts to kern, you are taking out the same amount of space between every pair of letters. This is a beginning process—you will still need to manually kern the characters for a perfect letterfit.*

Tracking

Tracking is a more complex issue. True tracking increases or reduces the letter spacing *according to the point size of the type.*

Remember when we talked about display type, and how the original metal letters were redesigned for large and small sizes, and that the spacing values were different for large and small type? Small type requires extra letter spacing; large type, as in headlines, requires less letter spacing the larger it gets.

Different applications use "tracking" differently. Adobe PageMaker, for instance, has true tracking: if you choose Normal tracking for very small type, PageMaker adds letter space; if you choose Normal tracking for large type, PageMaker subtracts space. It takes all the built-in pair kerns into consideration as well, so you get as close to optimum letter spacing as possible before having to manually fine-tune.

You might want to add PageMaker's tracking to your headline style sheet so all your heads have a start on proper letter spacing (you may still need to manually kern pairs of letters). You might want to track very small type so it has the tiny bit of extra space it needs. Because PageMaker's tracking is so thorough and complex, it's not a good idea to track large blocks of body copy—most body copy (9- to 12-point type) will not need tracking anyway. Reserve its power for large and small type.

The "tracking" in QuarkXPress is not true tracking; it is simply range kerning—it adds or subtracts a fixed amount of space between all letters selected regardless of kerning pairs or point size.

Find out exactly what your software does when you choose the tracking command. Whether it is true tracking or simply range kerning, understand what it does and use it when appropriate.

Kerning definitions

These are brief definitions of the variety of terms related to kerning.

What it is	What it means	Why use it
Letter spacing	Adding or decreasing the same amount of space between all the letters. Letter spacing is applied to a range of text; kerning is applied to individual pairs.	Usually used to change the spacing of a large amount of text to open the face or tighten it, depending on the natural characteristics of the typeface and its purpose on the page.
Kerning	General term for adjusting the space between letters.	Kern to create a visually consistent look.
Pair kerning	The special kerning built into certain combinations of letters when the typeface was designed. You can also use special programs to add more kerning pairs to your fonts.	This is built into your fonts— don't worry about it.
Auto kerning	When an application is capable of automatically finding and using the pair kerns built into the font.	You can turn auto kerning on or off in your application. Leave it on.
Manual kerning	Adjusting the fit of two characters by "hand" (computer "hand").	Use this for the final fine-tuning.
Range kerning	Selecting a range of text and applying an overall kerning value to all the pairs of letters.	Use this to tighten a range of text in preparation for manual fine-tuning.
Tracking	Means by which the computer adjusts the letter spacing, depending on the point size of the type and the auto kern pairs (PageMaker only; XPress "tracking" is really "range kerning").	Use this for large or very small type as a start for better letter spacing. For large type, you will still have to manually fine-tune the type.

Linespacing (leading)

Linespacing is the space between the lines of type. When type was set in metal (which wasn't that long ago), compositors would insert thin strips of lead between the lines of metal characters, which is why the space is called "ledding," not "leeding." Leading is measured in *points,* just like type. The measuring system works like this:

You take the point size of your type, say **12** point.
You take a (metaphorical) thin strip of lead, say **2** points.

12-point type You add the **12** points of the type size
+2 points of lead to the **2** points of lead, and you then say
=14 points of total that you have a leading value of **14** points.
space, called leading

This is written as **12/14** and is pronounced "twelve on fourteen."

The phrase **12/14** used to mean that text should be set at 12 point
and the typesetter should then drop down 14 points
to the next baseline,
but now it simply means that there are 14 points of space
surrounding the line of type,
and various applications
apply that space differently,
above and below the baseline.

Traditionally, an average leading is 20 percent
of the point size of the type.
Thus for 10-point type,
the average leading is 2 points,
added to the 10
for a 12-point leading value.
For 30-point type,
an average leading is 6 points,
for a 36-point leading value.

So now if you look at a type specification that calls for 10/16,
you instantly know there is a lot of space between the lines.
If you see type that is set with the same number for the
leading value as for the type size, such as 24/24, which is called
"set solid," you know there is very little space between the lines.

Not-so-average linespacing

Although 20 percent of the point size of the type is an average linespace, there are many times when you need to change that. Here are details of several clear-cut cases for when you *must* adjust linespacing, when you might *want* to, and a guideline for what to look at to determine the optimum linespacing for your text.

Headlines

If a headline runs two or more lines, you will probably need to decrease the linespace. The average 20 percent is okay for body copy, around sizes 9 to 12, but above that it starts to become excessive, especially when you get into sizes such as 48 and 72. Also in big headlines, take note of whether you have descenders or not, and where they fall. If there are no descenders, you really have to decrease the linespace.

The orchestra played egregiously   The orchestra played egregiously

Notice, above, how much extra space there appears to be between the lines, especially since there are no descenders in the first line. You can take out quite a bit of space, as shown in the example on the right.

The setting on the left is 18 point type with a leading value of 21.6, which is 20 percent.

The setting on the right is 18-point type with a leading value of 17 (which is actually what's called a "negative" amount of leading).

Typeface is Trade Gothic Bold Two.

All caps

When text is all caps, there are no descenders that drop into the line-spacing, but every one of the letters reaches up to the full height of the line. Because the words present such compact rectangles, you must be very conscious of the linespacing.

IN SMALLER SIZES, SUCH AS BODY TEXT (WHY WOULD YOU SET ALL CAPS IN BODY TEXT?), BE CONSCIOUS OF THE CROWDED FEELING THAT SOMETIMES HAPPENS WITH ALL CAPS—BE LOOSE WITH LINESPACING.

THE PARAGRAPH ABOVE IS SET WITH AUTO LEADING, WHICH IS 120 PERCENT OF THE POINT SIZE OF THE TYPE. IN THIS PARAGRAPH I ADDED A FEW EXTRA POINTS OF LINESPACE TO LOOSEN AND LIGHTEN THE LOOK.

In large sizes, as in big headlines, the compact words emphasize the amount of space between the lines; it can look disproportionate. You will probably want to decrease the space between the lines so the entire headline presents a compact package, rather than separate lines of packages.

THE DAYS ARE ENDLESSLY DULL

Eurostile Bold, 15/18

THE DAYS ARE ENDLESSLY DULL

Eurostile Bold, 15/16

If, for some reason, you need to set headlines or other large type in all caps, you will probably need to remove some of the linespace. Without the descenders, the space can appear to be excessive.

Sans serif text

Sans serif typefaces tend to have large x-heights. These large x-heights fill the space between the lines, almost always necessitating extra linespacing. But look carefully at the face first! Do you think this paragraph could use a little extra leading? Yes? You're right. This paragraph is set with the standard extra 20 percent.

Special effects

Sometimes you want to increase or decrease the linespacing dramatically for a special effect. Do it! Just make sure you do it with gusto. Don't just add a tiny bit more linespace—add a lot! Don't just make the text very tight between the lines—make it extraordinarily tight! If you are going for the effect, then go all the way. Don't be a wimp or it will simply look like a mistake.

Watch for these features

Large x-height:	Increase linespacing.
Small x-height:	Decrease linespacing.
Tall ascenders:	You can get away with less linespacing because the x-heights are relatively small, but you might want to actually add dramatic linespace to emphasize the tall ascenders.
Reverse type:	Along with increasing the point size by a point or two and increasing the weight a bit, you should probably also add a tiny bit more linespace.
Long lines:	If you must use long lines of text, add a tiny bit more linespace so the reader can find the beginning of the next line easily.
Wide letter spacing:	If the typeface is set with lots of letter spacing, add more linespace for balance.

Paragraph Spacing

The space between paragraphs is an important issue. Well, in the grand scheme of things I suppose it doesn't rank very high, but in typography it's important. If you space or indent your paragraphs poorly, your work belies you as an amateur.

First of all, let's clear up one thing: either indent your paragraphs *or* put extra space between them. Don't do both. The purpose of an indent is to tell the reader that this is a new paragraph. A small indent does that just fine. A small amount of space between the paragraphs does the same. But if you use *both* an indent and extra spacing, it's like hitting your reader over the head with a baseball bat because you think he is too stupid to read the clues for a new paragraph. He is not stupid. Choose one method.

Paragraph indents

So let's say you are going to indent your paragraphs. Are you going to indent them five spaces? One-half inch? No way. I know that's what your typing teacher taught you, and when you type across a page on a typewriter you probably need a five-space indent in proportion to the line length. But you are rarely setting lines that long on your computer, and besides, the standard typographic indent is one *em space*. An em space is a blank space as wide as the point size of the type; in 12-point type, an em space is 12 points; in 36-point type, it is 36 points. If you can set an indent with a measurement, set one em space. Otherwise fake it—an em space is more like two spaces than five.

Use your software to set the indent automatically. Word processors and page layout programs let you set a first-line indent; when you hit a Return, the text will start at wherever you set the first-line indent.

First paragraphs are not indented

The purpose of an indent is to warn the reader that a new paragraph is about to begin, right? Well, if it's the first paragraph, the reader does not need that clue—it's redundant. This is another one of those details where it might not look correct at first, but once you know it *is* correct and you apply it, other work will look foolish to you when the first paragraphs are indented.

Space between the paragraphs

If you want space between the paragraphs, *don't hit a double Return!* Learn to use your software to put an extra space after each paragraph, a space generally about half the amount of your linespace. If you hit two Returns you get a big gap, a gap that separates the very things that should be visually connected. The paragraphs on other pages in this book have a linespace (leading) value of 15 with 7 extra points of space after each paragraph.

But on this page I have hit double Returns. Aren't these huge spaces between paragraphs horrendous? It makes the work look so juvenile.

Again I must reinforce: learn to use your software. Every word processor and page layout application gives you control over the space between your paragraphs. Be smart. Look smart. Use it.

Alignment

The alignment of your text plays a vital part in the look and the readability of your work. It's not the only factor—typeface, line length, style, size, linespacing, and case (caps or lowercase) also contribute. Type that is easy and pleasant to read encourages people to read what is written. Type that is not so readable can discourage a significant portion of the audience.

In short text, as in an advertisement or a package design, you can often get away with using a design feature that detracts from the readability but adds to the attractiveness and impact of the piece (such as extreme letter spacing, or all caps with a justified alignment, or fringe type)—but this only works when you can justify that the *look* of the piece is more important than the accompanying loss of readability.

Passion without reason
is blind;
Reason without passion
is dead.

Will Durant
paraphrasing Spinoza

*A centered alignment
is very stable and secure
and tends to have
a more formal appearance.
It can be dull
because of this formality.*

Passion
without reason
is blind;
Reason
without passion
is dead.

Will Durant
paraphrasing Spinoza

*A strong flush right
or left alignment
has a clean edge
with an almost visible
line running along it.
The strength of this edge
adds strength to the design.*

Left aligned

Speaking just in terms of alignment, text aligned on the left is the most readable. Left-aligned text uses the optimum word spacing and letter spacing that the designer built into the font, and the spacing is very consistent so you don't have to struggle through the words at all. And as you read, your eye can quickly find the beginning of the next line.

When you align text left, strive to keep the right, "ragged" side as smooth as possible, or in a slightly concave shape. Sometimes this necessitates forcing line breaks to fill in holes or to prevent long text strings from hanging beyond the rest of the lines. Below, the word *of* is hanging off the right edge, while in the line just below it there is clearly plenty of room to accommodate the word. Bump *of* down to the next line (see Chapter 22 on Line Breaks for details).

If you bump words down, be sure you do it as the last touch in your final layout. Otherwise when you edit the text, change the type size or column width, or alter the layout in any way, you will end up with tab spaces, empty spaces, or line breaks in the middle of your sentences. Fortunately, in a flush left alignment you can easily make type corrections and adjust lines, often without affecting the rest of the text at all.

1. I declare! Sometimes it seems to me that every time a new piece of machinery comes in at the door some of our wits fly out at the window.
Aunt Abigail in *Understood Betsy,* by Dorothy Canfield Fisher

2. I declare! Sometimes it seems to me that every time a new piece of machinery comes in at the door some of our wits fly out at the window.
Aunt Abigail in *Understood Betsy,* by Dorothy Canfield Fisher

The word "of" in #1 will bump down to the next line, as shown in #2, but we get an even better "rag" by narrowing the entire paragraph just a tiny bit so the lines break as shown in #3.

3. I declare! Sometimes it seems to me that every time a new piece of machinery comes in at the door some of our wits fly out at the window.
Aunt Abigail in *Understood Betsy,* by Dorothy Canfield Fisher

Right aligned

Text aligned on the right creates a definite *look,* as shown below, quite different from left-aligned. The letter and word spacing still retain their ideal built-in settings, and corrections can often be made without affecting the rest of the text. The biggest drop in readability comes from the fact that the left edge, where your eye returns to find the next line to read, is not consistent so your eye has to find the beginning of the line again every time it moves to the left. In small amounts of text, this isn't a major problem, and the sacrifice can be worth it in exchange for the distinctive layout.

When you use a right alignment for the look it creates, then emphasize the look—don't be a wimp. Instead of keeping the ragged edge as smooth as possible, try exaggerating it.

There is no excuse for widows or hyphenated words when you set a right alignment. Since you are determining the line endings and since this for-mat is rarely used with an extended amount of text, you can help compen-sate for the lower readability by being thoughtful in the grouping of phrases. And while you're at it you can completely eliminate any hyphen-ation. Don't all the hyphenations in this paragraph look awful?

I'VE ALWAYS WANTED TO
BE SOMEBODY. BUT I CAN
SEE NOW i SHOULD HAVE
BEEN MORE SPECIFIC.
Lily Tomlin

*If you're going to align text
on the right, don't try to
disguise it. It's difficult to tell
if the text above is supposed
to be right-aligned or not.
Typeface is Las Bonitas.*

I'VE ALWAYS WANTED
TO BE SOMEBODY.
BUT I CAN SEE NOW
i SHOULD HAVE BEEN
MORE SPECIFIC.
Lily Tomlin

*If you make the right
alignment strong, it adds
another dimension to the
type and takes it beyond
merely words on the page.*

Center aligned

A centered alignment also gives a particular look to text: a more formal, sedate, and potentially more boring sort of look. People who are just beginning to work with text tend to center everything because it's safe. It's symmetrical. It fills the space, everything balances automatically. However, a centered alignment can create a dreadfully dull piece, and it often creates an amateurish page.

A centered alignment has consistent letter and word spacing, but you have to keep finding the beginning of the lines as you read so it is not the most readable arrangement. But if you're going to do it, then do it. Make it clear that the text is centered, not just poorly justified. Varying line lengths make the page visually interesting. Also, a centered alignment gives you a chance to group the lines into logical thoughts. And remember, there's never an excuse for hyphenated words.

On with the dance! Let joy be unconfined;
No sleep til morn, when youth and pleasure meet
To chase the glowing hours with flying feet.
Lord Byron

This is nice, but it doesn't have much strength or passion;
it's hard to tell the poem is centered.

On with the dance!
Let joy be unconfined;
No sleep til morn, when youth and pleasure meet
To chase the glowing hours
with flying feet.
Lord Byron

This layout has a much more intriguing shape.
Take advantage of the flexibility of centered lines.
Also read "Consider those phrases" on page 120.

Justified

When you justify text, the computer forces the lines to extend to a certain length by adding or deleting space between the words, and sometimes between the letters. Some programs let you specify the minimum and maximum amounts the spacing can adjust, but the computer will override your specifications if necessary.

The greatest problem with justified text, both in terms of readability and aesthetics, is the uneven word spacing and letter spacing: some lines have extra spacing, some less. This irregularity is visually disturbing and interrupts reading. The shorter the line length in relation to the size of the type, the worse this problem becomes because there are fewer words between which to add or delete space (see below).

One simple rule for determining whether a line length is "long enough" to justify is this: The line length in picas should be twice the point size of the type: if you're using 12-point type, the minimum line length before you should try to justify is 24 picas (6 picas equal 1 inch). This line length you are reading is 28p6 (28 picas, 6 points), and the type size is 11.6.

For many years, justified type reigned supreme as the way to set most text. But the trend over the past couple of decades has been to allow the natural spacing of flush left text to dominate, losing the structured look of the "block" of text, but maximizing readability.

So sweet a kiss the golden sun gives not to those fresh morning drops upon the rose, as thy eye-beams, when their fresh rays have smote the night of dew that on my cheeks down flows: nor shines the silver moon one half so bright through the transparent bosom of the deep, as doth thy face through tears of mine give light; thou shinest in every tear that I do weep.

William Shakespeare, *Love's Labour's Lost*

So sweet a kiss the golden sun gives not to those fresh morning drops upon the rose, as thy eye-beams, when their fresh rays have smote the night of dew that on my cheeks down flows: nor shines the silver moon one half so bright through the transparent bosom of the deep, as doth thy face through tears of mine give light; thou shinest in every tear that I do weep.

William Shakespeare, *Love's Labour's Lost*

Even with a long-enough line length, you will still get uneven word spacing when you justify the text. But notice how terrible the word spacing is in the example to the left—hold the page at an angle, squint, and you can see all the holes, and even "rivers" of white space running through the type. At least with a longer line, the gaps aren't so obvious. Typeface is Bembo.

Consider those phrases

I want to elaborate a little on the concept I keep mentioning: grouping words into phrases. We read and hear words in context, not as isolated items each with their own meanings. That is another reason all caps are hard to read—we have to read each word of all caps, but we understand whole clusters. Our mind has to work to put the individual words into those clusters.

Typographic beauty is a function of visual aesthetics combined with an intellectual assimilation. A page can look good with "greek" text or nonsensical combinations of words, but the type really packs a punch when the content (which is visible) is integrated into the design.

In the Durant quote on page 115, the visual impression is enhanced by the strong right edge. But it is also strengthened because of the phrases that are emphasized. With the flush right alignment, "without reason" and "without passion" are forcefully isolated, juxtaposed, and begging to be considered as a unit. The meaning of the words in these lines give more power to the whole piece. Always consider the phrasing when you have the opportunity to adjust it, as you do when your alignment is not justified or when the line length is short.

It's your choice

Choose one alignment per page—don't mix centered with flush left, for instance. With any alignment you choose, be aware of its strengths and weaknesses. Each alignment presents an initial visual image to the reader, has a different level of readability, and has particular quirks in regard to setting it. Evaluate these strengths and weaknesses, and base your decision on the combination of factors that best communicates your message.

In this book, I am obviously using justified type. The uneven word spacing bothers me, but because there are so many typefaces and type examples on these pages, I wanted the clean lines of a justified text block. It acts as a contrast to the extra stuff, and also as a solid, stable, repetitive background for the play of the other text. I was willing to make a conscious choice to justify the text and accept less-than-ideal word spacing in exchange for the clean lines of the edges of the paragraphs.

Details

*In which we explore
effective ways to
set headlines and
subheads, captions,
and pull quotes.
We also experiment
with various ways
to emphasize type,
and discuss the
importance of
sensitive line breaks
and hyphenation.*

Logic only gives man what he needs.
Magic gives him what he
wants.

Baba the
Idiot

Headlines and Subheads

The headlines and subheads in a document do more than simply give clues as to the content of the stories. They provide an organization to the page; they provide a repetitive element that unifies the publication; they provide the visual contrast that attracts our eyes to the page. Here are a few guidelines for using heads and subheads to effectively take advantage of their presence.

- Avoid using all caps or small caps. They are difficult to read, plus they take up too much space. Using lowercase letters, you will have more room to use a larger and bolder font.

- Watch the leading on multiple-line heads. The larger the type size, the less leading you need. If there are few or no descenders, it is particularly important to remove the excess space. Your intent is to keep the two lines together as one visual unit.

- If your text is flush left, keep your heads and subheads flush left, *not centered*. This is particularly important if your page feels a little cluttered; keeping the heads flush left with the text will reduce some of the visual clutter. When a head is centered, our eyes connect its placement with the first line of the first paragraph. If the first line of text does not stretch all the way across the column, the centered headline won't have a good connection to the story.

- To preserve the strength of this alignment (and to be typographically proper), don't indent the first paragraph in the story. Any indent you do use should be only about two spaces wide, about one em space (as wide as the point size of your type; see page 113).

> There should always be a little more space *above* a subhead than below it to ensure that the subhead is visually connected with the text it refers to. If the subhead is too far away, or if it is the same distance between the text above and below it, the subhead appears to be an unconnected, separate element.

> Create a clear distinction between heads and subheads. If the only difference between your head and subhead is size, then make sure they are significantly different sizes. You might want to italicize the subheads, or if you have a rule (a drawn line) beneath the headline, remove the line from the subhead.

> Always avoid awkward line breaks. Read your heads and subheads carefully for line breaks that might cause confusion or ambiguity, for silly line endings, and of course don't hyphenate.

> Choose a typeface for your heads and subheads that provides a strong contrast to your body text. This creates a contrast on the page that not only is visually attractive, but also strengthens the organization and makes a clearer path for the reader to follow.

Generally, your body text is a serif face, since extended amounts of text are easier to read with serifs. If so, a strong, bold sans serif is a good choice for heads and subheads. If you don't have a strong, bold face in your font library, you'll find that an investment in one is your single best investment toward more effective design and communication.

If your body text is a lightweight sans serif, the strong bold in the same font would work well for headlines. Just make sure there is a solid difference between the light weight and the heavy weight. For instance, the Helvetica Bold that comes on your computer is not bold enough to stand out effectively.

You might also want to consider a heavy slab serif face as a headline type, which is so different in structure and weight from any readable sans serif or serif that it works well as a headline type with almost any face.

Now that you've read through the guidelines, circle the appropriate places in the story below where you see the principles being used. Not every single guideline has been used in this one example, of course. How many do you follow in your work?

Giacche Enne Binnestaucche

Uans appona taim uasse disse boi. Neimmese Giacche. Naise boi. Live uite ise mamma. Mainde di cao.

Uane dei, di spaghetti ise olle aute. Dei gonna feinte fromme no fudde. Mamma sci sai, "Orai, Giacche, teicche di cao enne treide erre forre bocchese spaghetti enne somme uaine."

Giacche commes

Bai enne bai commese Giacche. I garra no fudde, i garra no uaine. Meicchese mesteicche enne treidese di cao forre bonce binnese. Uate giacchesse!

Mamma, scise engri. Giompe appe enne daonne craine, "Uara iu, somme caine creisi?" Denne sci tro olle binnese aute di uindo. Necchese dei, Giacche lucchese aute enne uara iu tincche? Ise si disse binnestaucche uate ricce appe tru di claodese. Somme uide!

Giacche gose appe di binnestaucche. Ise disse ogghere! Ise menne nainti sicchese fit taulle uite tri grin aise! Enne i garra ghusse uate leise ghode egghese!

Giacche ielle "Ciao!" Denne ise grabbe di ghusse enne cuicche claime daonne fromme di binnestaucche. Ise go cioppe cioppe uite di acchese. Di nainti sicchese futte menne ise faulle enne breicche di necche. Auce!

Cucchede ghusse

Mamma sci giompesse fromme gioi. Meicchese naise ghusse cacciatore. Bai enne bai, dei garra no morre fudde. Dei gonna dai! Uatsa iuse? Uara iu gonna du uenne iorre ghusse ise cucchede?

Many thanks to Michael Howley for passing this delightful story along to me!

Typefaces are Eurostile in the heads and subheads, Bembo in the body copy.

Have fun with it!

If appropriate for your content, experiment with different ways of setting heads. Perhaps add a rule above and/or below the heads, or reverse them, or set them extra large, or use an initial cap. If you have a special story, perhaps create a special headline. Keep in mind, though, that if every story has a special and different headline treatment, not one of them stands out as different or more important. Most stories should have typographically consistent headlines to retain the unity of the publication.

Always, always remember, your purpose is to communicate. No matter which technique you use, your heads and subheads should support that purpose.

Headline typeface is Mister Frisky.

Pull Quotes

Many times you must design or write a page that has no accompanying graphic to lighten the page and make it more enticing to read. That's where pull quotes come in so handy. A pull quote is when you take a quote from an article, story, or dull report and emphasize it on the page in some graphic way (as shown below). There are many ways to do this, and this chapter shows you several examples and provides some basic guidelines.

Pull quotes are often seen in the middle of the page, but there is no rule to force you to do this. Try some variations, such as a flush right or left quote in a wide outer margin (flush with the column of text); a quote in a background that cuts into one column of text; or a quote that runs horizontally across 1.5 or 2 columns. Use interesting punctuation marks, such as ampersands or questions marks, as graphic elements; perhaps set them large or colorful.

Evanescent wan think, itching udder.

On the following two pages are samples of pull quotes. Have fun with them, make them attractive—that's their point! Be sure to read page 130 for guidelines on working with pull quotes.

Be creative!

More often than not, the purpose of a pull quote is to add some visual interest to the page. So do it. Make that pull quote beautiful, provocative, interesting, dynamic!

"Wail, wail, wail," set disk wicket woof. "Evanescent Ladle Rat Rotten Hut."

A simple rule above and below the quote sets it apart. Notice the punctuation is hung off the left edge so the text retains its strong left alignment.

Typeface is Antique Olive Black.

You can't let the seeds stop you from enjoyin' the watermelon.

With a colored or black box, you can inset this quote so it tucks halfway into the adjacent column and hangs halfway out into the wide margin.

Typeface is Antique Olive Compact.

The harder you work, the luckier you get.

Tall, narrow settings with lots of linespace work well in outer margins. Align the flush edge with the edge of the column. That is, the quote in the outer margin of the left-hand page should be flush right, aligned against the column of text. On the outer margin of a right-hand page, the quote should be flush left.

Typeface is Bernhard Modern.

Ιν Δεχεμβερ α γυψ δελιϖερεδ α βυνχη οφ ωοοδ τηατ ηε χηοππεδ ιν μψ δριϖεωαψ. Ηε χηοππεδ τηε πιεχεσ τοο βιγ το τ ιν μψ στοϖε. Ηε σα ιδ ηε ωουλδ ρε τυρν ανδ χ ηο π τηεμ σμρ αλ λερ. Ηε νϖερ διδ. Ι παιδ ηιμ ρεπ εϖεν τηουγη ηε ασκεδ φορ Συ βεχαυσε ιτ ωασ α λοτ οφ ωοοδ ανδ Ι διδντ ρεαλιζε ηοω μανψ πιεχεσ ωερε υνυσαβλε φορ με. Σο ηε

She claims the secret to success is understanding that **your attitude is your life.**

σαιδ ηε ωουλδ βρινγ με α λοαδ οφ κινδλινγ. Ηε βρουγητ οϖερ ειγητ ρεδειγητ ρεδωοοδ ρουνδσ, εαχη αβουτ φερ 18 ινχηεσ λονγ ανδ φδτηρεε φεετ αχροσσ.

Ι κεπτ ωαιτινγ φορ τηε κινδλινγ ανδ ωηεν ϑιμμψ ναλλψ τολδ ηιμ Ι ωασ ωονδερινγ ωηερε τηε κινδλινγ ωασ, ηε σα ιδ τηε ρεδ– ωοοδ ωασ τηε κινδλινγ. Ιϖε βεεν ωονδερινγ

Try a horizontal quote extending across several columns. As with all pull quotes, leave plenty of white space surrounding it. Typefaces are Antique Olive Light, Antique Olive Compact, and Symbol.

To ensure success, learn to maximize your options.

Apply a gray shade or a pale color to large drop caps. This adds visual interest without overpowering the short quote.

Typeface is Belwe Medium.

Signifying the sound & the fury

Whenever possible and appropriate, take advantage of provocative punctuation and symbols.

Typeface is Antique Olive Nord with a Goudy Italic ampersand.

Guidelines for pull quotes

Here are a few guidelines for setting pull quotes in your documents:

- Always hang the punctuation (see Chapter 5).

- Reduce the size of punctuation in large type.

- Use only one alignment; for instance, don't set part of the text flush right and part of it centered.

- Make centered type obviously centered; break the lines at logical endings to create an interesting visual arrangement.

- Position initial caps on one of the baselines.

- Create a style for your pull quotes and use it consistently throughout your publication.

Captions

Captions are an important little feature of printed material. Every photo or illustrative figure should have an explanatory sentence or two accompanying it. People expect captions, so a photo without one confuses the reader momentarily. Often this explanatory text is the only thing people read. Take advantage of this fact, and don't let your captions be dull or useless—make them an integral part of the story and of the page design.

Choosing a typeface

The typeface for captions should either be a member of the same font family as your body text, or a font that is very different. Don't choose a font that is different but similar to the body text!

For instance, if you are using Garamond for your body text, feel free to use Garamond Italic or Semibold for your captions.

If you want to use another face altogether, choose something that is obviously different from your serif face, such as a sans serif—don't choose another serif. If you are using a sans serif typeface for your headlines, use a light weight of the same sans serif for the captions.

In my book, *The Non-Designer's Design Book,* the entire second half deals specifically with the problem of using more than one typeface on a page.

Choosing a type size and leading value

Captions are traditionally a bit smaller than the point size of the body copy, but keep in mind that many people read only the captions, so you don't want them to be difficult to read! Generally, use a size that is one to two points below the size of the body text (unless your body text is already tiny). If your body copy is 10 or 11 point, you can easily use 9- or 9.5-point caption type.

Alternatively, use the same size as your body text, but use the italic or semibold version of the font. You want it to be clear to the reader that these few lines are not meant to be in the flow of the story.

Your choice of leading value (linespace) depends on whether or not you are trying to align all your elements to a grid: Are you consciously aligning your baselines across columns? Are your headlines set in a linespace that is a multiple of your body copy linespace? For instance, say your body copy is 10-point type with 12-point leading. If your heads have a *leading value* (not necessarily point size of type) of 24 or 36 (two or three times the 12-point leading), all your text will always line up across columns, assuming you are indenting paragraphs instead of adding paragraph space between them. If so, your captions should follow the same guidelines—maintain that 12-point leading value.

If you are not forcing all elements into a grid format, then you have more flexibility with the leading value. Smaller type can usually get away with less leading. For instance, most faces at 9-point can get away with adding only a half a point or one point of linespace. Remember that sans serif faces need a little more linespace because their x-heights are usually larger than serif faces.

Alignment

Whether or not you are using a grid, the baseline of your caption should be on the same baseline as the text in the nearest column. The bottom of your photograph or illustration should also be aligned with a baseline in the next column. *This arrangement must be consistent throughout your publication!*

An even more important alignment is the relationship between the text and the photo or illustration. If your body copy is flush left or justified, then your captions should be flush left with the edge of the photo! Don't center captions unless everything else on the page is centered! You see, most photos have a strong, hard edge along both sides, yes? Your body text also has a strong hard edge along its side, yes? So don't weaken those clean lines by centering your captions—follow and increase the strength of those edges by aligning the caption with them.

Ms. Isabella Melanzana
will be speaking
at our next meeting.

▶ A strange figure was discovered
in the office late last night.

See the nice straight edge along the left side of this column? Follow that alignment with your caption! Don't weaken the entire page by centering your captions and losing the strength of that alignment.

Typeface is Memphis Light.

If you have some sort of detail you are using as a repetitive element throughout your publication, perhaps use it also in your captions. For instance, in the document from which the above graphic was taken, there are lists that use triangles as bullets. The triangle has been pulled into the caption as a unifying spark.

Typeface is Formata.

Be consistent

Whatever you're doing with your captions, be consistent. Don't confuse your reader; be thoughtful. Use the same alignment, typeface and style, size and leading. Be consistent about the placement—such as how far below the bottom edge of the photograph you place it, or aligning it with a baseline. Use a style sheet for the captions. (If you don't know how to use the style sheets in your application, you must learn! Style sheets are one of the most important features you can master.)

There are little tricks in every application for ensuring that the placement of captions is consistent—ask other people who use the same page layout application what tricks they use.

Emphasizing Type

Every page of type contains at least a few words or headlines that need to stand out, either because they are important to the content, or perhaps the words need to be emphasized to add enough visual interest to the page so a reader is attracted to it. No matter what the reason, there are appropriate and inappropriate ways to call attention to particular words.

DON'T DO THIS

The inappropriate ways of emphasizing certain words or phrases are generally holdovers from using the typewriter, when our only options were to type words in ALL CAPS or <u>underlined.</u> Rarely should you use all caps, and never should you underline. Never. That's a law.

When words are set in all caps, we lose the recognition of the shape of the word and are forced to read the word letter by letter (how many times have you read that now?). For instance, the word "cat" in lowercase has a different shape from the word "dog," and that shape helps us identify it. When the words CAT or DOG are set in all caps, their rectangular shapes are identical.

Italic, not underline

Typewriters, obviously, could not type in italic, so an underline on a typewriter was meant to fake an italic; that's why you were taught to type book titles with underlines, and why you underlined words in mid-paragraph when you wanted to emphasize them. But on your computer you have true typesetting choices—you don't have to fake it anymore, you can actually type in italic. Besides, the underline is usually too close to the bottoms of the letters and actually cuts into the descenders. And _<u>underlining</u>_ an italic word is simply redundant.

But you *can* do this

You have other options for emphasizing type that will create a more sophisticated or exciting typographic look, as well as help in the organization of information.

Using *italic* instead of an underline, where appropriate, is one way you can emphasize text in a subtle way, of course. For a stronger emphasis, use the boldest version of the typeface, or perhaps the ***bold italic.***

For a more dramatic emphasis, use a different typeface altogether, one that has a strong contrast to the rest of the text. For instance, if your text is a classic oldstyle face (like what you're reading right now), use a sans serif for emphasis. But don't use a weight that is *similar* to the other text, especially for headlines—notice how much more effective the **emphasis** is when the sans serif is a strong black.

If you have the opportunity to use another color, take advantage of that color in your text or headlines when you need an emphasis. Just remember that the less that second color appears, the more dramatic the emphasis will be. Warm colors (reds, oranges) are the strongest, and very little goes a long way. Cool colors (blues, greens) recede, and you can use more of them without overwhelming the page.

Add space

If your design allows, add empty space around the text to immediately draw more attention to it. I know, your boss doesn't like empty space—she says that she paid for it and she wants to use it. But think of those ads in magazines or newspapers where there is nothing at all except a few words in the middle of the page. Ask your boss if she noticed that ad. Ask her if she read that ad. Ask her if it is possible for anyone to open to that page and *not* read that ad.

No it is not.

The boss who had the courage to pay for all that space and let it be empty had the highest readership of any page in that entire publication. When there is clutter, our eyes are attracted to the resting places of the blankness. Have courage. Let the white space be there. Do you notice how much attention is called to that one line above, "No it is not"? It appears very important because of all the empty, white space surrounding it.

Rules and size can be effective

You don't ever want to use the underline feature in your software, but you can often apply a rule, or line, for emphasis, as shown in the headline above (in most programs you can add the rule to your style sheet so it shows up automatically). The advantage to the rule is that you can make it as thick or thin as you like, and you can make it a different color, dotted, or dashed. You can position the rule so it doesn't bump into the descenders, or, as you see in the running heads on each page, you can let it run through the descenders in exactly the position you choose.

Or:
Make it  Make it smaller!!

Of course you know you can emphasize type by making it bigger. But don't be a wimp—try making it *really* big, making the letterforms themselves into a design element, or perhaps enlarging just the interesting punctuation such as the question mark or ampersand or quotation marks. Or try setting the text very small, surrounded by lots of space. Either choice, large or small, will call a great deal of attention to itself.

So stretch yourself—go beyond the basic italic or bold word.

Line Breaks and Hyphenation

Your design project is all complete. Graphics are in place, colors have been chosen, paper has been selected, the service bureau is waiting for you, you think it's ready to go to the printer. But you need to check one last thing—your line breaks, or how each line of type ends. Yes, that means every line in your entire project, every headline, every caption, every line in every paragraph! Certain elements are inappropriate at the ends of lines, such as too many hyphens, small words that hang over an empty space in the next line, the last half of a hyphenated word as the last line of a paragraph, awkward phrases, among others. These are details that might not seem important at first, but these details are what gives a publication a professional appearance.

See, doesn't that paragraph look tacky?!

Yes, checking every line break can be time-consuming, but it will give your publications that added touch of professionalism.

How to fix line breaks

Sometimes the easiest and best way to fix bad line breaks, especially if they involve long words that are hard to manage, is to have editing privileges: change a long word to a short word, or a short word to a long one; rephrase the sentence; eliminate superfluous words. But since that is not always possible, here are a few tricks for adjusting the ends of your lines:

- Most software packages that work with text have a *line break* feature, sometimes called a "soft return." Instead of hitting the Return or Enter key, you hit Shift Return/Enter or perhaps Option Return or Alt Enter. This creates a hard line break, but it does not pick up any of the paragraph formatting you would get with a Return, such as extra space before or after, or a first-line indent or a style change.

- Most packages also have a *discretionary hyphen,* affectionately called a "dischy." You've probably noticed hyphens that occasionally appear in the middle of words in the middle of sentences (where someone manually hyphen-ated the word at the end of a sentence, later edited the sentence, and the hyphen stuck). Well, if you use a discretionary hyphen, usually by typing Command or Control Hyphen instead of the plain ol' hyphen, that hyphen will disappear when the word moves to another location.

  Also (and this is the point), if you *type a discretionary hyphen in front of a hyphenated word,* it will not hyphenate at all, ever. Use this to remove inappropriate hyphenations.

- You can often use subtle kerning or tracking in a line or in a few words, just enough to bring up the end of a hyphenated word.

- Try widening or narrowing the column just a tiny bit. Especially if it is set rag right, the difference won't be noticeable.

- For one-liners that are a bit too long, such as headlines or index entries or parts lists, try justifying the line. This will often squeeze ornery text onto one line.

What are bad line breaks?

Look for bad line breaks throughout every line of body copy. Of course, *do this only on final copy,* after all editing has been done! Here are several examples of the sorts of things to look for:

**Casing Adder ❶
Bat**

Heresy borsch-boil starry a ❷
boarder borsch boil gam
plate lung, lung a gore in- ❸
ner ladle wan-hearse torn
coiled Mutt-fill.

   Mutt-fill worsen mush of- ❹
fer torn, butted hatter putty
gut borsch-boil tame, an off
oiler pliers honor tame, door
moist cerebrated worse Cas- ❺
ing. Casing worsted sickened
basement, any hatter betting
orphanage off .526 (fife toe
sex). ❻

   Casing worse gut lurking
an furry poplar—spatially
wetter gull coiled Any-bally.
Any-bally worse Casing's
sweat-hard, any harpy cobble
wandered toe gat merit, ❼
bought Casing worse toe pore
toe becalm Any-bally's ❽
horsebarn. (Boil pliers honor
Mutt-fill tame dint gat mush
offer celery; infect, day gut
nosing atoll.)

   Butt less gat earn wetter star- ❾
ry.

Casing Adder Bat

Heresy borsch-boil starry
a boarder borsch boil gam
plate lung, lung a gore inner
ladle wan-hearse torn coiled
Mutt-fill.

   Mutt-fill worsen mush
offer torn, butted hatter putty
gut borsch-boil tame, an
off oiler pliers honor tame,
door moist cerebrated worse
Casing. Casing worsted sickened basement, any hatter
betting orphanage off .526
(fife toe sex).

   Casing worse gut lurking
an furry poplar—spatially
wetter gull coiled Any-bally.
Any-bally worse Casing's
sweat-hard, any harpy cobble
wandered toe gat merit, bought
Casing worse toe pore toe
becalm Any-bally's horsebarn.
(Boil pliers honor Mutt-fill
tame dint gat mush offer celery;
infect, day gut nosing atoll.)

   Bought less gat earn wetter
starry.

❶*Justify the headline so it stays on one line.* ❷*Use a line break (Shift Return/Enter) to bump "a" down to the next line, where it fits very nicely.* ❸*Kern the line a tiny bit to bring the rest of the word up.* ❹*Type a dischy in front of the word to bump it down.* ❺*Never hyphenate a person's name. I had to go up a few lines, bump "off" down, which bumped the other line endings down. This also took care of the inappropriate widow in* ❻*.* ❼*There is plenty of room to squeeze "bought" on this line, perhaps by kerning the line a tiny bit.* ❽*"Horsebarn" is a good long word that could be hyphenated; type a dischy. Better yet, when "bought" moved up, it gave enough room to move "horsebarn" up. If not, try opening the text block or text box a wee bit.* ❾*Edit: to get rid of that terrible widow, exchange a short word for a long word.*   Story is by Howard Chace.

Headlines

Don't hyphenate headlines. That's a law.

Don Quixote de la Man-cha

Don't laugh—I have actually seen this as a printed headline. Someone did it.

Also, watch where the first line of a two-line headline ends—does it create a silly or misleading phrase? Fix it.

Professor and The-rapist to Lecture

Don't Lose Your Self Respect

Don't leave widows (very short last lines) in headlines.

Man Walks Barefoot Across Bay Bridge

Fix it either way, or rewrite!

Man walks barefoot across Bay Bridge

Man walks barefoot across Bay Bridge

Captions

Generally captions don't need to stretch all the way across a column width. This flexibility gives you the freedom to break lines at appropriate places to create sensible phrasing. This is especially true if you center captions—you don't want all the lines the same length anyway.

Breaking sentences into complete phrases creates a more readable caption, and since many people read only the captions, it behooves you to make them as readable as possible.

Will Rogers said, "We can't all be heroes because someone has to sit on the curb and clap as they go by."

Why hyphenate in a caption?

Will Rogers said, "We can't all be heroes because
someone has to sit on the curb and clap as they go
by."

There is no excuse to leave a widow in a caption!

Will Rogers said, "We can't all be heroes because someone
has to sit on the curb and clap as they go by."

Will Rogers said, "We can't all be heroes because
someone has to sit on the curb and clap as they go by."

*These last two would not look good as paragraphs, but
would work fine aligned under a photograph or illustration.*

Hyphenation

If your text is flush left, right, or centered, hyphenation isn't a big problem. The only rule is to watch out for too many hyphens in a row and word breaks that are too short. Personally, my preference is never to allow more than one hyphenation in a row, and preferably no more than one in a paragraph. Other people whose opinions I respect are comfortable with, say, no more than three in a row. Also personally, I abhor those hyphenations that leave one or two letters at either end of the line. Others don't mind. No one, however, finds a hyphenated word as the last word in a paragraph to be acceptable.

If you are going to *justify* your text, you have other considerations to weigh because the computer hyphenates words in an attempt to maintain the most even word spacing possible. It's impossible have totally even word spacing in justified text—the computer has to unnaturally force words to the beginnings and ends of the lines.

There are two schools of thought on justification with hyphenation: Some people are willing to put up with lots of hyphenated words, including two-letter ones, to ensure that the word spacing is as even as possible. Others are willing to accept uneven word spacing in exchange for fewer obnoxious hyphens at the ends of lines—hyphens that interrupt the flow and color of the text much more than does a subtle change in or less-than-ideal word spacing. Guess to which school I belong? Guess which paragraph on this page makes me twitch with horror?

You can set your page layout application to get the effect you want. I have Adobe PageMaker set to not allow hyphenations that would occur within three picas of the end of the line (depending on the length of my line), thereby eliminating two-letter breaks, and to not allow more than one hyphen in a row. In QuarkXPress you can get even more specific. In both programs you can add the hyphenation controls to your style sheets.

Special Effects

In which we experiment
with ornaments
and dingbats,
swash characters,
initial caps, and
black-and-white "color"
in type, as well as
effective ways of using
distressed typefaces.

In mAtters
of grave importance,
STYLE
not sincerity,
is the
Vital thing.

Oscar Wilde
The Importance of Being Earnest

Swash Characters

Have you ever wanted to give an extra-special look to some type without being too bold? Perhaps you want a strong yet elegant look? A judicious use of swash characters can add a touch of sophistication to headlines, titles, quotations, etc.

Swash characters are specially designed letterforms that have "tails" or elaborate shapes, usually swooping away from or under the rest of the letters. Swash characters are like cheesecake—use them sparingly for a delectable (not disgusting) effect. In the three examples below, the first one is the regular face, the second is the italic version, and the third is a combination of the italic and its matching swash font.

Name that Tune   *Name that Tune*
Name that Tune

Swash characters are not included in a regular font character set—you must buy a specially designed font in conjunction with your text font. For instance, the typefaces used above and in the first two examples on the next page are Zapf Renaissance Light and Light Italic, with a special swash face designed to complement them called Zapf Renaissance Light Italic Swash. You need to use the faces in combination with each other. It's common to use the italic swash with the regular face as well as with the italic face.

Many swash faces also contain a set of ornaments which can be used to complement the type. Their proportions and style are designed to work smoothly with the text. Several of them are used in this chapter, but also see Chapter 26 for details on ornaments and dingbats.

Guidelines for using swashes

There are a few guidelines to remember when working with swash characters:

- Please, don't *ever* set text in all capital swash characters.
  OH MY GRACIOUS THIS LOOKS SO STUPID.
  Besides looking stupid, it is also dreadfully difficult to read.

- Swashes are designed to add elegant curves *to otherwise empty spaces,* such as under or over letters, or at the ends of sentences. So don't insert the kind of swash in the middle of a word that creates an unsightly gap, or even at the end of a word in mid-sentence if it disturbs the word spacing.

  Her specialty was analyzing goblins.

- In a typeface that imitates handwriting, swash characters can add to the effect of a personalized note, making it look handlettered. Below, the typeface General Menou includes many alternate and swash characters (notice the alternate characters for d, s, e, and g, among others). But don't limit a handlettered face such as this to only personal notes! General Menou is so beautiful it could easily be used for any elegant occasion.

  Dear John,
  I miss you. Wish you could have dinner with me tonight at Rancho de Chimayó, with dessert in front of the fire and the snow falling outside.
  Love, R.

- If you are going to use another typeface on the same page as the swash face, be very careful. Avoid faces with similar characteristics, such as any other italic or script. Either stay in the same family, such as the Zapf Renaissance family, or choose a font that has strong contrasts (such as thicker strokes or a roman or sans serif or monoweight font).

- Don't overdo the number of swashes. As you've seen, the swash characters add elegance only if they are used with discretion.

- It helps to have a utility such as the control panel PopChar, available for the Mac in a free version or in a shareware version. Download it from the web at **www.shareware.com**. Or use Adobe's KeyCap. On a PC, use the Character Map. See Appendix C for details about where to get these items and how to use them.

Don't be a wimp

Don't be shy! If you find a swash or two that is exceptionally beautiful, set it extraordinarily large and use it as a graphic element on your page—show it off! Set it in a pale color or a shade of grey and let it swoop under your body text or behind a photograph. Use a huge swash character as an initial cap or as a lead-in to an article or chapter. Combine one large italic swash character with heavy, bold, black sans serif characters for a striking contrast in a title or quote. Look through this book and take note of where and how I've used swash characters. Oh, the possibilities are endless and exciting!

Lord, what fools these

Mortals be!

William Shakespeare,
A Midsummer Night's Dream

Initial Caps

LARGE OR ORNATE LETTERS at the beginning of first paragraphs, also called initial caps or drop caps, not only add interest to a page, but help guide the reader's eyes and pull the reader into the text. There are many ways to create an initial cap, as shown in the examples following. Be brave, be strong, be big where appropriate. Here are just a couple of simple guidelines to remember.

- The baseline of the initial cap or the bottom of the graphic image belonging to the initial cap should align with one of the baselines of the text.

- Don't overdo it. One initial cap is beautiful; an initial cap beginning every paragraph on the page is redundant and destroys the effect. Sometimes on a text-heavy page you can use two or three initial caps in lieu of graphics or pullquotes, but be aware of their impact and don't overdose the reader.

For only the very young
saw Life ahead, and only
the very old saw Life behind;
the others between were
so busy with Life
they saw nothing.

Ray Bradbury

Typeface is Isadora.

Examples of initial caps

There is a wonderful variety of ways to use initial caps. Here are several examples, which I hope will inspire you to play and create even greater and more interesting ways to use them.

Sometimes the seas are calm, and that's wonderful. Sometimes the seas are not calm, and that's the way it is.
Rabbi Nathan Seagull

Typeface is Bodoni Poster Compressed.

In PageMaker, I set the letter "O" in a text block of its own, then selected it with the pointer tool and grouped it (yes, I grouped it by itself). Then I was able to wrap the text wrap around it. Typeface is Schmelvetica.

O time, strength, cash, and patience! Small erections may be finished by their first architects; grand ones, true ones, ever leave the copestone to posterity. God keep me from ever completing anything.   Herman Melville, Moby Dick

I set the "W" separately from the text. I moved the text over using hard spaces (em, en, and thin spaces). Typefaces are Belwe Condensed and Light.

When I'm in a good space, I see obstructions as instructions. When I am in a bad space, even instructions look like obstructions.
Norm Howe

In the midst of all the doubts which we have discussed for four thousand years in four thousand ways, the safest course is still to do nothing against one's conscience.

Voltaire

Typefaces are Printers Ornaments M for the decorative block, ExPonto Multiple Master for the cap "I" and byline, and Decon Struct Medium for the body copy.

Letters sometimes give ear to a disturbing tremor which seismically runs the gamut of the entire alphabet. They are plagued by the lascivious laughter of the old satyrs of the woods and the painful cries of the dying. In the valleys of rich abundance and in their dwelling house, the atmosphere seems to them suffocatingly oppressive.

One unforgettable night they quit with light abandon the heavy encumbrance of words to seek the wordless heights where the air is purer and the horizon infinite. They have been freed by the whim of a capricious god. The great silence of the heights feels like a soothing caress across the feverish brow . . . they have reached the top of the mountain and fulfilled the longing of a lifetime.

But, should they remain there until the dawn streaks the sky, they will be torn to pieces by the wolf of abstractions. In a frightened, concerted mass, they rush down the slopes, bleating miserably. Only when they reach the sanctuary of the pen do they feel happy and secure.

One of them, however, stands with its nose pressed between the bars of the closed gate; it is the O, longing to return to the mountain heights.

Olof Lagercrantz

If the text is rather playful, experiment with lots of initial caps. Experiment with pale colors or tints, and don't let them overwhelm the body copy. Try letting the pale initial caps slide under the text above them, as on page 151. Typefaces are Eurostile Bold Condensed and Caslon Regular.

Notice I kerned the cap "T" out to the left a little so its stem aligned with the cap "I" in the next line. Typeface is Bernhard Bold Condensed.

**Take it as it comes.
If it doesn't come, go get it.
If you can't get it, create it.**

The ditches were rushing rivers; the ponds were full, the earth was already turning green, the swish of the rain upon the trees was terrific; but deafening, drowning all other noises was the ecstatic chorus of millions of frogs from every ditch and pond and field and compound, a wild, mad, maddening, corybantic, croaking and creaking orgasm of sound of wet, wallowing frogs.

Leonard Woolf

Typefaces are Fantasia Initial Caps for the cap "T" (which is actually an EPS file) and Dirty One for the body copy.

Automatic drop caps

 n both PageMaker and QuarkXPress you can apply drop caps (one form of initial caps, as shown below) automatically. You can tell both applications how many lines you want the letter to drop down. In Quark, you can specify up to eight letters to act as drop caps in the first line. (The drop cap in this paragraph is Massele, from the set of EPS initial caps called Initial Caps III from Adobe Studios. They have a wonderful variety of sets.)

In **PageMaker,** use the "Drop Cap" plug-in from the Utilities menu.

In **QuarkXPress,** look in the Formats dialog box under the Style menu. You can add a drop cap to a style sheet, which can be a wonderful and useful thing.

Also take a look at the initial letters offered by many font vendors. Many come as graphics in EPS format (as the one shown in the first paragraph, above), which means you can text wrap them, color them, or resize them endlessly. There are some incredibly beautiful caps to choose from—get a set and see what they inspire.

E verything must end. Meanwhile, we must amuse ourselves.

Voltaire

This is a drop cap created instantly in PageMaker using the drop cap feature. Typeface is Jim Casual.

Typographic Color

Typographers have always referred to black-and-white type on a page as having "color." It's easy to create contrast with colorbox colors; it takes a more sophisticated eye to see and take advantage of the color contrasts in black-and-white. Often, black and white are the only "colors" available, but don't let that limit you—this chapter will give you some ideas to use to ferment your own.

A gray, text-only page can be very dull to look at and uninviting to read. I'm sure you've opened up newsletters or technical documents and found these dull pages, or perhaps you've had to create them. It's not always possible to have graphics on a page to break up the text, but something needs to be done. A gray page can also create confusion by not giving the reader any clue as to the importance of a story or whether two separate stories on the page are related to each other. An effective typographic technique to aid in the organization of a page is to add "color."

Just as the voice adds emphasis
to important words,
so can type:
it shouts or whispers by variation of size.

Just as the pitch of the voice
adds interest to the words,
so can type:
it modulates by lightness or darkness.

Just as the voice adds color
to the words by inflection,
so can type:
**it defines elegance, dignity, toughness
by choice of face.**

Jan White

It's pretty easy to see what is creating the different colors in the typefaces above. Not only is it the weight of the stroke, but also the structure of the letterforms: tall and condensed vs. long and squatty. Also notice the color of the lightweight text in the example compared to the body copy in the paragraphs above. Typefaces are Eurostile Condensed and Eurostile Bold Extended Two.

What makes "color"?

The color of a typeface is determined by a combination of details: the space between the letters and between the lines, the space built into each character, the x-height, the thickness of the strokes, the serifs or lack of serifs, etc. A light, airy typeface with lots of letter spacing and linespacing creates a very light color (and texture). A bold sans serif, tightly packed, creates a dark color (with a different texture). You can clearly see the contrast of colors in the samples below.

In the time of your life, live . . . so that in that wondrous time you shall not add to the misery and sorrow of the world, but smile to the infinite delight and mystery of it.
William Saroyan
Caslon Regular 8.5/10.5

In the time of your life, live . . . so that in that wondrous time you shall not add to the misery and sorrow of the world, but smile to the infinite delight and mystery of it.
William Saroyan
Decon Struct Bold 8.5/9.5

In the time of your life, live . . . so that in that wondrous time you shall not add to the misery and sorrow of the world, but smile to the infinite delight and mystery of it.
William Saroyan
Nuptial Script 10/10.5

In the time of your life, live . . . so that in that wondrous time you shall not add to the misery and sorrow of the world, but smile to the infinite delight and mystery of it.
William Saroyan
Memphis Medium 8.5/9

In the time of your life, live . . . so that in that wondrous time you shall not add to the misery and sorrow of the world, but smile to the infinite delight and mystery of it.
William Saroyan
Bernhard Regular 8.5/12

In the time of your life, live . . . so that in that wondrous time you shall not add to the misery and sorrow of the world, but smile to the infinite delight and mystery of it.
William Saroyan
Jimbo MM 8.5/10.5

In the time of your life, live . . . so that in that wondrous time you shall not add to the misery and sorrow of the world, but smile to the infinite delight and mystery of it.
William Saroyan
Regular Joe 8.5/10.5

In the time of your life, live . . . so that in that wondrous time you shall not add to the misery and sorrow of the world, but smile to the infinite delight and mystery of it.
William Saroyan
ExPonto Light MM 8.5/10.5

In the time of your life, live . . . so that in that wondrous time you shall not add to the misery and sorrow of the world, but smile to the infinite delight and mystery of it.
William Saroyan
Flyer ExtraBlack Condensed 8.5/10.5

2 5 : T Y P O G R A P H I C C O L O R . **157**

Why use black-and-white color?

If you add color to your heads and subheads by using a typeface with a heavier weight, or if you perhaps set a quote or a passage or a short story in an obviously different "color" (as in a pull quote), the page becomes more visually appealing. If it's visually appealing, readers are more likely to stop on a page and actually read it. And that's the point, right?

Besides making the page more inviting to read, this change in color also helps organize the information. Below, which of the two arrangements gives you an instant visual impression of what's going on, as opposed to having to read the actual text to see what the organization is?

Center Alley
Center Alley worse jester pore ladle gull hoe lift wetter stop-murder an toe heft-cisterns. Daze worming war furry wicket an shellfish parsons, spatially dole stop-murder, hoe dint lack Center Alley an, infect, word orphan traitor pore gull mar lichen ammonol dinner hormone bang.

   Oily inner moaning disk wicket oiled worming shorted, "Center Alley, gad otter bet an goiter wark! Suture lacy ladle bomb! Shaker lake!" An firm moaning tell gnat disk ratchet gull word heifer wark lacquer

hearse toe kipper horsing ardor, washer heft-cistern's closing, maker bets, gore tutor star fur perversions, cooker males,

washer dashes, an doe oily udder hoard wark. Nor wander pore Center Alley worse tarred an disgorged!

Hormone Derange
O gummier hum
warder buffer-lore rum
Enter dar enter envelopes ply,
Ware soiled'em assured
adage cur-itching ward
An disguise earn it clotty oil die.
Harm, hormone derange,
Warder dare enter envelopes ply,
Ware soiled'em assured
adage cur-itching ward
An disguise earn it clotty oil die.

With this page being so dull and gray, it is not instantly clear whether there are two separate stories, or perhaps they are both part of the same one. And the page has no contrast to attract your eyes.

Typefaces are Caslon Regular and Bold.

Center Alley
Center Alley worse jester pore ladle gull hoe lift wetter stop-murder an toe heft-cisterns. Daze worming war furry wicket an shellfish parsons, spatially dole stop-murder, hoe dint lack Center Alley an, infect, word orphan traitor pore gull mar lichen ammonol dinner hormone bang.

   Oily inner moaning disk wicket oiled worming shorted, "Center Alley, gad otter bet an goiter wark! Suture lacy ladle bomb! Shaker lake!" An firm moaning tell gnat disk ratchet gull word heifer wark lacquer

hearse toe kipper horsing ardor, washer heft-cistern's closing, maker bets, gore tutor star fur perversions, cooker males,

washer dashes, an doe oily udder hoard wark. Nor wander pore Center Alley worse tarred an disgorged!

Hormone Derange
O gummier hum warder buffer-lore rum
Enter dar enter envelopes ply,
Ware soiled'em assured
   adage cur-itching ward
An disguise earn it clotty oil die.
Harm, hormone derange,
Warder dare enter envelopes ply,
Ware soiled'em assured
   adage cur-itching ward
An disguise earn it clotty oil die.

The "color" now does two things: it attracts your eyes to the page, and makes it clear that there are two separate stories. Can you see what is creating the different "colors" of type?

Typefaces added are variations of Eurostile.

Stories are by Howard Chace.

Color as in crayons

"Color" is a term with various interpretations, one of them, obviously, being color. When you are using actual colors, like those in a crayon box, an important thing to keep in mind is that warm colors (reds, oranges) come forward and command our attention. Our eyes are very attracted to warm colors, so it takes very little red to create a contrast, to catch your eye, to lead you around the page. It is easy to overdose on warm colors by applying too much in too many places. I know you paid for that second color, but I guarantee it will be more effective if you use it in small doses. I also know it is hard to convince your boss of that. Find examples of where color has been used sparingly to great effect and keep those examples in a file. Also find samples of color being used obnoxiously. I have a newsletter in my file that uses a second color of an ugly red—this ugly red covers over half of the newsletter, defeating the purpose of using color to make important items stand out.

Cool colors (blues, greens), on the other hand, recede from our eyes. You can get away with larger areas of a cool color; in fact, sometimes you *need* more of a cool color to create an effective contrast on the page. But even with cool colors, if the point of the color is to emphasize a point or to add a sophisticated splash, less is usually more.

Scribble some red color in this little shape. Hold the page up and glance at it. Where does your eye land first? Tiny spots of color are powerful.

Ornaments ❧ and Dingbats

❧ Ornaments and dingbats are delightful and easy ways to add visual interest to your pages. They are simply little decorative elements you can set along with your type because they are characters in the font. ❧ Some fonts, especially expert sets, have ornaments as extra characters. You can also buy entire sets of them as typefaces. ❧ What's the difference between ornaments and dingbats? It's a fuzzy line, but you might say that dingbats are the sorts of little elements you would use as bullets, whereas ornaments are more sophisticated decorations for more elegant type. But then again you might also say the two are the same. ❧ One use for ornaments or dingbats is as you see here—markers that indicate new paragraphs without actually making a paragraph space or indent. This can be an interesting effect for a short amount of copy, but more than one page of it would be difficult to plow through. ❧ Notice I added more linespace to this page, in addition to the ornaments; this was to lighten the color (see the previous chapter) and give a more inviting, open look to this solid block of text that really should be several short paragraphs. ❧

Oh for a Muse of fire, that would ascend
the brightest heaven of invention.
William Shakespeare, Henry V

Other uses for ornaments and dingbats

Here are several other ideas for using ornaments. Once you own a font or two of dingbats and ornaments, you will discover all sorts of places to throw them in. Don't be a wimp.

- It is very common to see an ornament at the end of a magazine story indicating the end of that article. If you decide to use this technique, be consistent with the ornament so the reader knows what to expect when they see the mark.

- Use ornaments in pull quotes to set the text apart, as on the previous page. This can be a beautiful and interesting alternative to a simple rule (line).

- Also experiment with using special dingbats as bullets in a list of items, or in a row as a border.

- Try throwing playful dingbats into your memos, letters, faxes, and other correspondence. There is no excuse for being dull.

- Use a repetitive pattern of dingbats as a background texture, as shown below. Because the dingbats are a font, you can easily resize them, space them, and adjust their linespacing to make the pattern as light or dense as you like.

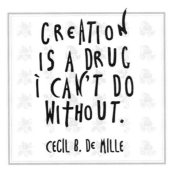

CREATION
IS A DRUG
I CAN'T DO
WITHOUT.
CECIL B. DE MILLE

Typeface is Pierre Bonnard.

Pi and Picture Fonts

Pi (pronounced "pie"), pictograph, and picture fonts are similar to ornaments and dingbats (see the previous chapter) except that they tend to be more specific. Many smaller vendors provide these specialty fonts that don't enjoy a large market, and they are often just what you need for a particular project. There is a font for just about everything. If you need a specialty font, order the catalogs of the smaller vendors (check Appendix A at the back of this book for vendor addresses).

Pi fonts

A pi font is a special typeface with mathematical and scientific characters, indispensable for use in technical manuals or scientific treatises. What a blessing these fonts can be! And beyond the obvious practical use, many of these characters are interesting symbols that can be used in other ways. If you have one, print up all the characters and keep your eyes open for creative new ways to use them.

What would you do if you needed these characters and didn't have this font! Typefaces are Mathematical Pi 5 and Mathematical Pi 6.

These come in so handy when writing technical manuals. There is also a companion font to this set that displays all the other keys, such as Shift, Control, Command, and the rest. Typefaces are PIXymbols Stylekey and PIXymbols Function.

Pictograph fonts

Similar to pi fonts are pictograph fonts, which provide international symbols. Many of these symbols are so interesting that they beg to be used in ways you might not immediately think of: in logos, perhaps, or as identifying organizational symbols in a brochure or annual report, or as decorative elements on their own.

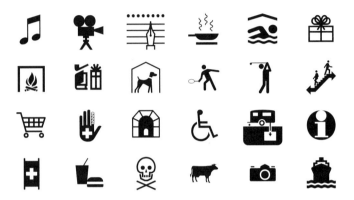

If you ever need symbols like these, check out the fonts. You can always open the font in Macromedia Fontographer and customize it. Typefaces are PIXymbols Hotel and PIXymbols Travel.

Instant logos!
Typefaces are Jimbo Multiple Master, Isadora (script),
PIXymbols Travel (pictograph).

Picture fonts

Picture fonts, where each character is a little picture, can be used in oh so many ways. Similar to dingbats, you can use them as bullets. Or instead of a dotted or dashed line, try a line made of a picture font character or a combination of characters. Use them as borders, as clip art, as custom art. You can make them very small, add space between them, or even change their color easily.

Picture fonts are great for quick, easy, and inexpensive logos. You can enlarge a picture character to the maximum size in your program, sometimes as large as 18 inches. You can change their color, condense or expand them, kern them, and build them right into the text of the logo. If you know how to use a program like Fontographer from Macromedia, you can customize the character and still use it as easily as you would the letter A.

The character shown on the left, from the picture font Printers Ornaments M, had the right feel but slightly the wrong look for the intended logo. I opened the font in Macromedia Fontographer and just moved a few points to give the character more female lines, as shown on the right. The other face is Eurostile.

These fonts are so much fun to collect and use everywhere. Drop pictures into memos to your boss, love letters, signs, business cards, t-shirts— have fun! Typefaces are MiniPics Lil Ancients, Birds, and MiniPics Doohickies Too.

You can create interesting borders out of many picture fonts. Typeface is MiniPics Doohickies Too.

Rebus stories

And when you run out of things to do, gather your kids, a couple of picture and pi fonts, and create a rebus story. Although the stories are generally pretty silly, I guarantee the process will make you laugh, and that's a valuable thing.

ONCE upon a time there was a little 🏃 who had a 🐕 named fido. one ☀ day the 🐕 chased a 🐈. this 🐈 had just caught a 🐭. the cat's friend was having a birthday party with a 🎂 and the 🐈 was bringing this dead 🐭 as a birthday present. before the 🐈 could get to the 🏠 for the party, the 🐕 started chasing him. a little 🐦 saw the predicament and jumped in his new red 🚗 and sped off to get his friend the 🐟 who really couldnt do anything to help and so the 🐕 ate the 🐈 who had killed the 🐭 on this ☀ day and that was that.

Typeface is Hansel, which includes the letters and the pictures.

Note!

When you print picture and pi fonts, make sure the button "Use Symbol font for special characters" is not checked or you will print the wrong symbols! It's in your Print dialog box somewhere.

Don't be a Wimp!

ype has just recently become a household item. The media tells us that people are reading less and less, yet type is becoming more and more important. How many typefaces could you name ten years ago? How many do you now have on your computer? How many billboards, book covers, t-shirts, and ice cream containers do you now look at and wonder what the typeface is?

As a result of this increased awareness of typography is increased power and strength of printed words. Everyone is more conscious of the words—not just what they say, but how they are presented. Type is art, but art with a clear purpose. The next chapter talks about evocative typography, and about choosing typefaces that reinforce your message. But in this short chapter I simply want to exhort you to take full advantage of this new typographic consciousness. It is so easy to make your pages alive, exciting, provocative—but never forget that your purpose is to communicate.

Extremes

Don't be afraid to go to extremes. Find ways to use type extremely large or extremely small, at least in proportion to the piece. I recently received a letter with the name and address of the sender in some really funky type at least two inches tall. It had an incredible impact—full of chutzpah and creativity. In phone book advertising, newspaper ads, brochures, flyers, in many, many places, try using extraordinarily large type. A good contrast would be to have the body of the piece in a decently small size, say 10 point. Don't think that because the heading is so large that the rest of the type has to be larger than average also—no no! It is specifically that strong contrast between the large and the small that makes the piece so effective.

White space

It's okay to have white space, empty space on your page that is not filled with text or graphics or anything but clean empty space. It's okay. You can do it. Your type will love it. When you find type treatments that appeal to you, take a moment to see where that designer let the white space be. Chances are there is a fair amount of it. Look through this book at all the white space. Look through other books and see how much white space they have, and be conscious of your reaction to the ones that have very little. Be brave enough to let the empty space just sit there. It's okay.

Odd typefAces

There are so many wonderfully offbeat typefaces available—oh my my my! Once you get up the nerve to use them, you'll find they are appropriate in many more ways that you might have first thought. If you're a little shy, start off using them on projects for which you don't have clients, such as postcards to friends, invitations to your daughter's birthday party, flyers for your lost dog, the family chore list, your Christmas letter, or as graphic text on your web page. Once the odd typefaces become part of your repertoire, sneak them into a memo to your boss—just one word for now:

Memo   MEMO   Memo   MEMO

She'll hardly notice. Start infiltrating it around the office—notices in the lunchroom, minutes to the meetings, instructions in the restrooms. It is a sad fact of human existence that we tend to fear what we don't know, so make your favorite wild font a local, familiar face. Everyone will become friends and then you can introduce it to your stationery and business cards. Ha!

Typographic Choices

In which we explore typefaces that evoke a response from the reader, Multiple Master technology, tips on choosing a typeface, trends in type, and desktop publishing pitfalls.

Watzlawick's First Axiom of Communication:

You cannot *not* com-municate.

Paul Watzlawick

Evocative Typography

Evocative typography refers to a choice of typeface that reinforces the message of the words, type that evokes a desired response. Designers have always been very careful about their choice of type, and I know you have been through that process many times. You have a definite idea of which faces would be appropriate for different projects. You wouldn't make a Garage Sale sign in German blackletter. You wouldn't do a brochure for a construction company in a delicate script. What I want to accomplish with this chapter, though, is to encourage you to push the concept of evocative typography even further than you have been, and also to take a closer look at what you are evoking. If the first thing that comes to mind for a Japanese tea garden festival is a typeface made out of little pagodas, toss it. Corny. Consider what symbolizes the festival—grace, beauty, tradition? Perhaps try a lovely oldstyle with graceful curves, set large so you can enjoy its beauty. Do some research, discover that the most popular typeface in Japan for many years was Baskerville, a transitional oldstyle—try that. Maybe you need to do a flyer for the children's museum. Your first thought is to use a hand-scrawled typeface with backwards characters. If the flyer is for kids, try using real letters instead of cute lettering that reinforces backwards letters. Try New Century Schoolbook, which was designed for children's books, or a clean sans serif that emulates the way children write their alphabet. You can always use picture fonts to add playful illustrations all over the page.

Next time you need to decide on a typeface that reinforces the text, think it through carefully. Don't always go with your first idea. Since we are on computers, it is so easy to play with all of our options, to change faces with the click of a button. Typefaces are cheap now—invest in a variety! Remember, you can never have too much money, too much RAM, or too many fonts.

Easy choices

Some choices will be very easy, some you will have to think about. The ones below are easy—circle the typeface that would probably communicate the message best for each of these examples:

Lost Shih-Tzu Puppy!   *Fette Fraktur*

Lost Shih-Tzu Puppy   *Carpenter*

Lost Shih-Tzu Puppy!   *Aachen Bold*

TOULOUSE-LAUTREC SHOW OPENS FRIDAY   *Pierre Bonnard*

TOULOUSE-LAUTREC SHOW OPENS FRIDAY   *Karton*

Toulouse-Lautrec Show Opens   *Prestige Elite*

'6"2 W,LLY'S ,P'c, KU\P FO\R \SA⌐LE   *Gladys*

'62 Willys Pickup For Sale   *Franklin Gothic Heavy*

'62 Willys Pickup For Sale   *Nuptial Script*

More difficult choices

Many of the choices you will have to make are not so easy (unless you only have six fonts on your computer). Push your creative process, think about what you really mean, play with visual puns, make people think about what they read.

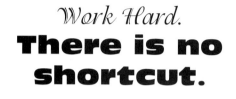

*I'll bet these type choices bother you. I'll bet you think "Work Hard" should be the phrase in big, solid, bold type. Well, y'see, it all depends on your point of view and what you want to express. In my life, this is how I see it: ya work hard. **THERE IS NO SHORTCUT** (please excuse the all caps). That's the way it is— it's a fact of life that you work hard. What is difficult to get through my teenagers' heads is that **there is no shortcut.** Typefaces are Isadora and Antique Olive Nord.*

So how would you quit? It might depend on the job and the circumstances, of course. Maybe one day you would quit in ❶ *Marie Luise and another day you would quit in* ❷ *Clarendon. Maybe your boss drives you to quit in* ❸ *Chicken. I can tell you that most any day I would quit in* ❹ *Shelley Volante, with a sassy smile on my face and my fingers toodle-ooing goodbye. See ya later, alligator!*

Think it through

If you have something important to say and you want to reinforce the message with typography, think it through very carefully. There is a place for platitudes. Sometimes the most obvious solution is the best, just as the trite phrase, "like looking for a needle in a haystack" is very clear—a reader can make no mistake about what you mean. All of our tired phrases have a reason for being true—we get it. We get the point. We see the connection. We understand the analogy. So there is also a place in typography for the old saws.

But don't neglect the beauty of a new turn of phrase, a new way of expressing an old thought, a new twist on a tired idea. Sometimes it will behoove you to probe a little deeper, think about the project, and write down the various ideas you are trying to project. Look at your type choices carefully—the more you work with type, the more you will become conscious of the details that project an image.

It is not just the details of the typeface that create a response, it is how you use it. Say you choose a tall, narrow modern to project a sophisticated, highbrow appearance to the ad for your small store. Emphasize that tall and narrow with a strong flush right or left with narrow line lengths, perhaps lots of linespace, maybe a trendy ornament or two.

Keep a file of graphic design pieces that created a strong response in you— good or bad. Take a few moments to put into words how an appropriate response from the reader was created: note the details, the alignments, the white space, and the combination of typefaces. In pieces that evoked an inappropriate response (different from what you think they wanted), figure out where the contradictions are—the typeface, the linespace, the angles, or other details? *The more you are able to see and put these things into words, the more control and power you have in designing your own work.*

Keep your eyes open, and be conscious!

Multiple Masters

Are you ready for more choices? Are you ready for the potential to customize miniscule characteristics of your fonts with the touch of a slider bar? Are you ready to turn a serif font into a sans serif font, or create a hybrid, with the click of a button?

At this moment in history we can manipulate a font in one direction: size. Some software lets us also expand or compress the type, which just stretches or squishes the characters. Or we can choose to use expert sets (see Chapter 8) that include display fonts for optimizing large type sizes. But each of these is an electronic patch emulating what a dedicated typecutter or type designer used to belabor.

When a designer creates a font, she usually designs a bold weight to go along with the regular weight, and perhaps an expanded or condensed version. Each of these variations has subtle differences in proportions, subtle weight changes in the strokes, letterfit, and white spaces. When we arbitrarily choose to electronically condense a face, rather than use the condensed version the designer created (maybe because one doesn't exist), we don't get those variations, those subtleties that are built in to enhance readability. We get a squished version (see Chapter 12).

Adobe Systems' font technology called Multiple Masters, has an interesting solution to this problem. A multiple master font can be manipulated in more than one dimension and can be minutely and automatically customized to solve typographic problems such as rivers and widows and unwanted hyphenations. The difference between tweaking your existing type the way you have been doing it and using a multiple master is that *the multiple master font will retain the correct proportions and stroke width changes.*

Design axes

The multiple master technology uses from two to four design axes. When you buy a multiple master font, on the box you will see how many axes it has. Most of them have only two, width and weight, although more and more are being created with the third axis, optical size.

Let's say you have a font with only one axis, width. Picture a very light-weight, condensed letter in one corner. Horizontally across, in another corner, is a very lightweight but extended letter. In the tiny squares between are all the letters that make that transition from condensed to expanded, each properly designed. But they're not really there yet—that's your job. You move the slider bar and the new font is created.

B B B B *This is a small sample of the width access possibilities. You can create hundreds of variations in-between.*

If the font has the weight axis as well, visualize a checkerboard with tiny squares. In the top left and right corners are the matrices for the design axis, weight, as described above. Imagine that in the vertical corner below the light condensed letter there is a very bold condensed letter. And in the fourth corner is a very bold expanded letter. Again, you can create any of the characters between the two. This is another design axis, the weight axis.

Now imagine all the tiny little squares on the entire checkerboard filled in, interpolated between both the weight and the width axes. You can choose any variation of a character with any combination of weight and width. Remember, the difference is that these letterforms retain their intrinsic design characteristics.

B B B B *You can create hundreds of variations in*
B B B B *any direction between the four corners, as*
B B B B *bold and fat as the bottom right corner, as*
B B B B *light and narrow as the upper left corner,*
                                    and anything in-between. Amazing.

Optical size axis

Some multiple master fonts also include optimizing, or visual scaling, capabilities. Remember Chapter 13 on display type, and how the design characteristics are different for large-sized type than for small type? Well, some multiple master fonts have a third design axis, size, with a small point size at one end and a large point size at the other, each designed for maximum readability and legibility. You can choose to interpolate any type size between the two, which theoretically means that any size type will have beautifully proportioned, properly spaced characters.

If you think of the first two design axes weight and width as being on a checkerboard, then these three design axes are a three-dimensional checkerboard. The top and bottom layers of the board have the same weight and width axes, but the top layer is a tiny point size and the bottom layer is a large point size and in-between are all the different sizes along with all the variations in weight and width. Oh my gosh.

So if a font has all three of these design axes (weight, width, and size), you can adjust the weight and the width of your type and still keep the proportions beautiful and readable as you enlarge or reduce the text.

Style axis

And there is a fourth design axis (the fourth dimension?) of style. At one end is a sans serif font and at the other end is a serif font. The style transitions from monoweight, unstressed letterforms to a typical serif, two-weight form. Or perhaps the style ranges from inline to decorated, or from a slab serif to a face with wedge serifs. Not every multiple master font encompasses all four design axes. In fact, very few encompass this fourth axis yet.

Font emulation and ATM

Multiple masters have another amazing feature: they can automatically emulate the font metrics of any font they must substitute. Have you ever created a document on one computer, then opened it on another computer to find that the formatting was completely destroyed because the same font was not available? Well, if you have a multiple master font to substitute for the missing one, the multiple master would pick up on the font metrics—the spacing, the letter widths, the kerning values, etc.—so the document would retain the same line breaks, page breaks, paragraph depths, and all the other type formatting even though it is a different font. When you take the document back to your own computer, the font changes back to the original one. Amazing. This is the technology behind what used to be called SuperATM and what is now built into current versions of ATM (Adobe Type Manager). If you have ATM installed properly and you use Adobe fonts, *it works automatically—ATM substitutes appropriate fonts for you on the fly and makes them fit.* Oh, it is truly remarkable.

Generating multiple masters

In some **Macintosh** applications, including Adobe PageMaker and Quark-XPress, you can generate new multiple master "instances" with the click of a couple of buttons. Once you have any multiple master font installed (they have an MM after their names), this is how easy it is:

> **Adobe PageMaker (Mac):**
> From the Type menu, choose "Character...."
> From the font list in the dialog box, choose a multiple master typeface, then click the button "MM Fonts...."

> **QuarkXPress (Mac):** From the Utilities menu, choose "Font Creator."

> ❧ **Then in either application:** From this dialog box, which is the Font Creator (as shown below), choose any of the multiple master fonts you have installed. Move the slider bars around until you see the font as you like it. Click OK. A new "instance" of the font will be instantly created for you and will appear in your font menu.

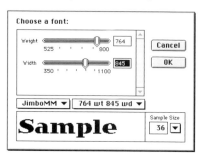

This is how simple it is to create a new instance of a multiple master font. Just drag the slider bars; the sample on the bottom shows you what the new instance looks like. Click OK and it's in your menu and thus ready to use in any application, not just the one you created it in.

If your Mac application doesn't work directly with multiple masters through the font menu, Font Creator is found as a stand-alone utility on one of your multiple master font disks. Read the manual! It's only one step more difficult than doing it directly in the page layout application.

On **Windows,** it's just as easy—create new "instances" directly in Adobe Type Manager. See Appendix C for more details.

The instances you create will not be named in a way that makes sense. As you can see in the example, I created an instance of Jimbo that will appear in my menu as "764 wt 845 wd." This means that on a scale from 525 to 800 in weight (as you can see in the dialog box), I have chose 764. On a scale from 350 to 1100 in width, I have chosen 845. Once you are conscious of the scale for the font, you can picture the relative look of the typeface when you see those numbers in the font menu. The larger the numbers, the heavier the strokes and the more stretched the letterforms.

Why would you want to create Multiple Master faces?

Multiple masters come in handy in so many places. You can easily adjust a headline to fill the space without having to change the size, or you can make reverse text a little bolder so it will hold its shape. Perhaps you have a ticket or a poster that needs a wide range of weights and widths and sizes for all the various parts of the information. Maybe your grandma complains that the font in the letters you write her are too light and thus difficult for her to read—so fatten up the strokes, maybe also widen them a bit.

Eventually you will be able to do things like select the type in your headline and tell it to fill the space, or select the text that runs over a bit too much and tell it to resize to fit the space—the multiple master will create a new instance to do the job, maintaining the integrity of the design and its readability and legibility. Oh, life is so exciting.

Can you see the eight different instances of this font, Tekton MM, used in this card? It can be incredibly valuable to be able to create real fonts in various weights and widths.

Don't try to go to that web site or cafe—it's gone. Sigh.

Choosing a Typeface

WHAT TYPEFACE SHALL I USE?
THE GODS REFUSE TO ANSWER.
THEY REFUSE BECAUSE THEY DO NOT KNOW.

W.A. Dwiggins

Dwiggins' cry to the gods is one with which we are all familiar. Even though there are more than 10,000 typefaces available to us, finding the perfect font for a particular job can be a stressful task. Or more likely it is *because* we have 10,000 fonts to choose from that the task often appears monumental. There are steps you can take, though, to narrow the selection down to a handful of appropriate choices.

Remember those categories of type?

First of all, remember those general categories of type you read about in the beginning of this book? And remember the sections on readability and legibility? Understanding those categories and concepts is important in helping narrow your choices, so let's review them.

Oldstyle faces have slanted serifs, gradual thick-to-thin strokes, and a slanted stress (the O appears tilted). The original oldstyle faces were created for books, so they are eminently readable.

Modern faces have thin, horizontal serifs, radical thick-to-thin strokes, and a vertical stress (the O does not appear to tilt). If there is more than a paragraph or two of a modern face, the strong thick/thin contrast in the letterforms creates a "dazzling" effect that makes moderns less than perfectly readable. The more pronounced the contrast in the stroke, the less readable in extended text.

Slab serif faces have thick, horizontal serifs, little or no thick/thin transition in the strokes, and a vertical stress (the O does not appear to tilt). If the slab serif is not too heavy, it can make a very sturdy and solid readable face.

Sans serif faces have no serifs, and almost all sans serifs have monoweight strokes (no thick/thin contrast at all). The absence of serifs and the monoweight strokes make sans serifs slightly *less readable* than oldstyles, but because they have such clearly defined letterforms without the addition of little diddlies like serifs, this style is actually *more legible* than serif faces in short bursts of text.

You probably need no review on what defines a typeface as **script, decorative,** or **fringe**—they're pretty self-explanatory.

And do you also remember reading about **readability** and **legibility?** The more distinctive features, the *less* readable it is, the less suitable for long blocks of text. The oldstyle category and the light weights of slab serifs are the *most* "invisible" and subsequently the most *readable.* Sans serifs tend to be more *legible* because they have clean, straightforward letterforms.

Questions about your project

To narrow the choices of faces for a project, here are questions to ask yourself. The questions are not ranked in order of importance—each one is a critical consideration. Consider these three options together:

What is your output printer resolution:
Low (72–144 dots per inch),
Medium (300–600 dpi), or
High-resolution imagesetter (1270–2540 dpi)?
Are you going straight through a fax machine
(consider it low resolution)?

What will be the final reproduction method:
Copy machine, quick press, high-quality press?

On what kind of paper will you be reproducing the project:
Newsprint, cheap bond, textured stock, glossy stock, fax paper?

Quality

The common thread between these questions is *quality*—the quality of the type itself that comes out of the printer, the quality of the reproduction method, and the quality of the paper. If each of these variables is on the high end, then you can use any typeface you choose as far as technical reproduction is concerned. If any of these variables is on the low end (or on textured paper, even though it's high quality), you need to be more selective to make sure your type will reproduce well.

Less than very high quality

- Type from a lower resolution printer cannot retain subtle design characteristics, such as very fine lines or delicate serifs.

- A copy machine or a fax machine also loses some of the fine details in the reproduction process.

- Inexpensive paper, especially newsprint, absorbs ink and loses even more, sometimes to the point of filling in the counters (those spaces inside letters like **e** or **d**).

For any of the poorer conditions, choose a typeface that has sturdy serifs, no fine lines, and a larger x-height with open counters, such as those shown below. Most sans serifs will hold up very well under any conditions. Also look through font catalogs for typefaces with these characteristics.

Clarendon Plain or Clarendon Light
New Century Schoolbook
Bookman
Memphis

All of these faces have solid strokes and serifs that will not fall apart under difficult printing conditions.

Is there an extensive amount of text to read?

If you have an extended amount of text, as in a lengthy newsletter, an annual report, or a book, you need a body typeface with maximum readability (remember Chapter 2?). Under the best printing conditions (high resolution output, smooth paper, and a good printing press), try a classic oldstyle for best readability. You are reading Caslon Regular right now, which is a classic oldstyle.

Under the worst printing conditions, try a typeface in the slab serif category that will still be extremely readable but will not fall apart in the reproduction process.

This typeface would give you a headache in a long body of text. In fact, don't you find it difficult to read even in this short bit? Great for headlines:

Hats off to you!

This typeface will hold up well even under the worst conditions, is clean and orderly, has a business-like presentation, and would be quite readable in extensive text. This is Clarendon Light. **It also comes in this Clarendon Plain** which is a little heavier, **and this Clarendon Bold for a great and sturdy impression.**

Compare reading these two samples, plus the two paragraphs above the samples. Do you get a feeling for which are easiest to read? Once you are conscious of it, the details that make a typeface readable become obvious. Typefaces are Bodoni Poster Compressed on the left, Clarendon family on the right.

Are you cramped for space, or do you need to fill space?

You've probably noticed that different typefaces take up different amounts of space, even at the same point size (see page 16 on the anatomy of type). The most critical factor for this difference is the width of the characters. Times has an average x-height, but the characters are slightly condensed to fit more on the page. Other faces, such as Garamond, are more round and open and fill a page easily. Plus, if a typeface is open, it also likes to have extra line spacing and wider margins to complement its spaciousness, which you can take advantage of to further fill the space.

There are entire books of type which display paragraphs of text set in a wide variety of fonts. By comparing the paragraphs you can see which fonts can fit more text in a given space at a given size. Check your local public library or college library for type books.

Even though the two paragraphs below are both set in 10.5-point type, Times takes up less space than Garamond. You can imagine if you had many columns of type!

14-pica line

The loss of the state of innocence in which Baskerville looks like Bembo, and Helvetica is indistinguishable from Universe, has the compensating advantage that we become more aware of the tiny details and the 'subtle allure' which go to make up the best faces.
Sebastian Carter

Times 10.5/13

14-pica line

The loss of the state of innocence in which Baskerville looks like Bembo, and Helvetica is indistinguishable from Universe, has the compensating advantage that we become more aware of the tiny details and the 'subtle allure' which go to make up the best faces.
Sebastian Carter

Garamond 10.5/13

Is the purpose of the piece rather sedate, or can the text be a little playful?

Sometimes even when there is a fair amount of text, as in a brochure, you don't want or really need an invisible typeface. There are many typefaces that are certainly readable enough for short text, but also distinctive enough to create a look that emphasizes your message. Realize you are making a choice between ideal readability and an impression, and get as playful as you like as long as you can justify your choice.

A casual look versus a serious look

❶ I'm sure you already have a sense of which typefaces appear more casual and informal than others, but noticing exactly what kinds of features create that look gives you more strength behind your choices.

❷ *Casual faces tend to be more distinctive; their features often have quirks. Rounded, soft edges make it more comfortable; serifs that curve or branch off at odd angles give it a friendly twitch. Faces that resemble handlettering or handwriting of course have a casual feel. These quirky or softened features are comparable to wearing red cowboy boots or sneakers—they create a distinctly casual impression no matter what the words themselves say.*

❸ The typefaces with a more professional, or serious and stable look are the "invisible" faces I mentioned in the readability chapter, the ones that simply communicate clearly with no quirks. These are the gray suits of typography, the bastions of respectability, the guys in the mold.

So which of the three paragraphs above is the gray suit, which is the evening gown, and which is the t-shirt?

Typefaces are Bernhard Modern, Improv, and Caslon Regular.

Is the project to be skimmed or really read?

In a job like a catalog or parts list where the reader will primarily be skimming headlines to find the text they want to read, keep in mind that sans serif faces are more legible, meaning the separate character forms are more easily distinguished at a quick glance (as long as they are not set in all caps!). You are also more likely to find condensed versions of sans serif faces, which are often necessary in the kind of piece where you're trying to get a lot of information onto the pages. And a sans serif will hold up well under the often less-than-ideal printing conditions of many catalogs or parts lists.

If the sans serif catalog headlines are meant to lead readers into *paragraphs* of text, consider using a serif face for the paragraphs, both for maximum readability and for visual contrast.

HEADS
Storage for the mind.
Available in many sizes
and preferences.

SHOULDERS
Come in broad, narrow,
strong enough to carry
the worries of the world.

KNEES
Choose from knobby,
knock, bad, or weak.

TOES
Order ten at a time for
the most comfortable fit.

EYES
Wide range of colors.
Can choose an attitude
to go along with.

EARS
Everything from small
and sweet to large and
winglike.

WAISTLINES
Whatever you order,
take care of it as they
tend to disappear as
you get older.

Heads
Storage for the mind.
Available in many sizes
and preferences.

Shoulders
Come in narrow, broad,
strong enough to carry
the worries of the world.

Knees
Choose from knobby,
knock, bad, or weak.

Toes
Order ten at a time for
the most comfortable fit.

Eyes
Wide range of colors.
Can choose an attitude
to go along with.

Ears
Everything from small
and sweet to large and
winglike.

Waistlines
Whatever you order,
take care of it as they
tend to disappear as
you get older.

So what is making the second list easier to read, and making the heads easier to scan?

- *Upper- and lowercase instead of all caps.*

- *Extra space above each head.*

- *Contrast with the body copy.*

- *Sans serif for heads (Formata Bold), serif for body copy (Garamond Light).*

Evocative typography

Notice these questions don't even address the subject of whether a particular typeface suits your job emotionally; that is, whether the look-and-feel of the face itself reinforces your message. I do hope you read the chapter on Evocative Typography for my opinions on this most interesting of typographic questions. Within the limits of your reproduction process, push your creativity here. Experiment with new and different faces, faces you might not have considered at first. Don't analyze them—get your gut reaction. Keep your eyes open for what others have done, consciously clip examples of unusual type choices and file them for later inspiration. You'll be surprised at what can work!

DECORATIVE AND FRINGE FONTS

There are so many wonderful and wild typefaces now, with more being created every day. Obviously, these intriguing fonts are for special occasions, but what occasions! Just be careful not to overdose your reader with too much of a special face—its strong impact will be diluted. Rather than use a uniquely creative face for all the headlines in your newsletter, save it for one very special article. The contrast between the stable headlines and the wild one will give your special article more impact.

Headline typeface is Erosive.

An exercise and method

I recommend you call the phone number in every font ad you see, call all the vendors listed in Appendix A in this book, and go to all their web sites, and request their catalogs of typefaces. Spend a few minutes looking carefully at each face in the catalog and try to place each one into one of the general categories of type. Once you have found its basic place (many will not fit neatly into a category—that's okay, just get as close as possible), then make some judgments. Does it have distinctive features or is it invisible? Does it wear red cowboy boots or a gray suit? Does the face have fine, delicate features that might not hold up through a fax machine, a copier, or on textured or cheap paper? Or does it have sturdy features that can go through the wash?

Analyze your project

- Know your output method and final reproduction process, and narrow your choices down to appropriate faces that will retain their design qualities. (Reread, if necessary, Chapters 2 and 3 on readability and legibility.)

- Decide on the look you want to convey, then narrow your choices to the distinctive or the invisible (or a combination that is exciting and still readable).

- If you use more than one face, make sure the fonts are decidedly different from each other. If you have chosen a beautiful oldstyle for the body text, try a bold sans serif for headlines. (If you haven't yet, you might want to read another book of mine, *The Non-Designer's Design Book*. The second half of the book focuses on the specific issue of combining typefaces.)

- Don't be afraid to use wild fonts where they are appropriate, and remember they are most effective (as is any rich item) when used sparingly—the richer, the more powerful. But don't be a wimp!

THE GOOD THING IS THAT
WE HAVE SO MANY FONTS.
THE BAD THING IS THAT
WE HAVE SO MANY FONTS.

Telltale Signs of Desktop Publishing

Desktop publishing has matured from the original classic ransom notes that we were inundated with in the mid-1980s. People have become much more visually aware and informed about the professional way to set their own type and design their own pages. But telltale signs of do-it-yourself desktop publishing creep into even the most professional work. Some of these signs are a result of not knowing the software well enough to control certain features, and some are simply evidence of using convenient features that really shouldn't even be options — or, in some cases, defaults — on the computer.

Give yourself three penalty points for each of the following telltale signs that you perpetrate. If you score three or above, you lose.

1. Helvetica

Type has trends, just like hair styles and clothing and eyeglasses and architecture. Helvetica was the most popular typeface in the world in the '60s, and in the '70s it was a way of life. By the '80s Helvetica was becoming as passé as beehive hairdos and then it appeared in the Macintosh font menu and then in the PC font menu. Just as a beehive hairdo creates a certain look, Helvetica creates a certain look. A dated look. A '70s look. Just because it's on your computer doesn't mean you have to use it. The greatest thing you could do for your publications is to invest in another sans serif face, one with a strong, bold black version in its family. As with all trends, Helvetica will someday be back in style—in about two hundred years.

This is Helvetica—groovy, man.
Try anything else: Trade Gothic, **Formata, Antique Olive,** Eurostile!

2. Straight quotes

It is amazing that after all these years people are still typing straight quotes. Learn the keystrokes to type real quotes, and in every application you use, take advantage of the feature that types them for you automatically (read your manual!). But don't type curly quotes when you need inch and foot marks (in fact, use prime marks; remember Chapter 4)! And don't type an opening quote at the beginning of a word that really needs an apostrophe! And put the quotation marks and apostrophes in the right place!

"Can you believe that dog stands 7'3" tall? Its huge!"

"Can you believe that dog stands 7'3" tall? It's huge!"

Notice the prime marks for the numbers, and the quotation marks are hanging!

3. Double returns

Hitting the Return or Enter key twice between paragraphs or after headlines separates the text with big, awkward gaps. Double Returns also make it possible to end up with a blank line at the top of a column.

Learn to use "Paragraph space after" and the "Paragraph space before" feature—it's in every program that uses lots of text. With that feature you can determine exactly the amount of space you want between paragraphs, after headlines, above subheads—an elegant space that tells the reader a new paragraph has begun without physically separating the text so much.

Notice the difference between these three paragraphs and the rest of the paragraphs in the book—wouldn't you agree that the gap appears unnecessarily large?

4. Two spaces after punctuation

I know, I know—if you are still typing two spaces after periods it is probably because you firmly believe it looks better that way. If all the work you create is for yourself, go ahead and continue to type two spaces. But you would be doing your clients a disservice to set *their* type with two spaces after periods because by now most people have become visually astute enough to notice the unsightly gaps created by that double space. Publications typed with two spaces have an unprofessional appearance, whether you agree with it or not, and your work will be ridiculed. Open any novel on your shelf—see any double spaces? Did you read that novel and complain to yourself that you couldn't tell where the sentences ended? The high-quality type you are using, with its proportional widths and kerning pairs that tuck the letters so close together, does not need two spaces to separate sentences. Squint at this paragraph—notice any holes?

5. Gray boxes behind text

Just because you *can* make gray boxes doesn't mean that you have to. Beginners often use gray boxes to make important parts of the text stand out because they don't have other ideas about how to make type a focal point, or at least make it a little more important than average. Besides screaming "amateur," type on that dotted, gray background is difficult to read. (Even worse are gray boxes with rounded corners. I know you have a tool for making rounded corner boxes. So.)

If you want to make a portion of the text stand out, try something else: a dramatic headline font, reverse bold heads, heavy rules (lines) above and below the article, extra space around the type. Keep your eyes open and see what others do—copy those ideas!

Warning:
Do not touch the red knob while cleaning this machine or you will detonate the blasting cap and the machine will explode.

Besides looking plain ol' dumb, the dots that make the background gray also make the text difficult to read.

Warning!

Do not touch the red knob while cleaning this machine or you will detonate the blasting cap and the machine will explode.

White space, heavy and thin rules, bold typeface—oh, so many ways to call attention to text without using gray boxes.

6. Centered layouts

Centered type creates a stable, sedate, formal look because it is so symmetrical and balanced. It can also create a deadly dull look. New designers center type because it is a very safe thing to do. If you center the page because you *want* a more formal look, that's one thing. But if you center the page because you simply haven't thought about it, or because you are afraid of uncentering it, that's another thing. As you flip through any magazine, stop at the layouts that interest you. Most of the pages and ads that have a strong, dynamic feeling are not centered. An invisible line connects the elements in a flush left or flush right alignment, and the strength of that line gives strength to the entire page.

If you are going to center, then do it with gusto. Don't try to make all the lines similar lengths; instead, show off the fact that it's centered. And if you're going to center, center *everything*—don't stick something in the right-hand corner just to fill the corner. Corners don't mind being empty.

I think and think for
months and years. Ninety-
nine times, the conclusion
is false. The hundredth
time I am right.

Albert Einstein

*Mmm, nice and boring. And the
typography in no way reinforces
the message of the text.*

I think and think
for months
and years.
Ninety-nine times,
the conclusion is false.
The hundredth time I am right.

Albert Einstein

*What did I do
to this centered arrangement
to make it a bit more
dynamic?
Name five things.*

*Typeface is Optima Plain, Bold,
and Oblique.*

7. Borders around everything

One border around a page often indicates a beginner who feels unsafe with type that is uncontained. The more boxes of type with borders around them, the more insecure the designer. I know, it feels safer to box it in; it gives the type a place to *be,* without just floating in the space. But y'know what? It's okay to let it be. Really. That white space (the "empty" space) is itself a border—it encloses the type, yet lets it breathe; it defines the edges, yet maintains a freedom.

8. Half-inch indents

Yes, I know your typing teacher taught you to indent five spaces or one-half inch, but that was for a typewriter. Typically on a typewriter you were typing all the way across the page, and the type was relatively large.

A standard typographic indent is one em space, which is a space as wide as the point size of the type. In 10-point type, an em space is 10 points wide; in 36-point type, an em space is 36 points wide. This is roughly equivalent to *two* spaces, not five. Especially when your type is in columns, a half-inch indent is way out of proportion.

9. Hyphens for bullets

- Using hyphens as bullets is a typewriter habit, and it looks dumb in professional type.
- The round dot bullet (•, type Option 8) is a little better, but experiment with more interesting bullets.
- You can get strong little squares or triangles out of Zapf Dingbats, or play with other picture fonts. Make them smaller and use the baseline shift feature to raise them off the baseline (read the manual!).
- It's amazing how this little touch can add more sophistication to a piece. See Chapter 26.

10. Outlined shadowed type

Type that has been outlined and shadowed by the computer still shows up, and in the most surprising places (like book covers, billboards, and annual reports). Don't do it. If you're just starting to use your computer, I know the temptation is great because with the click of a button you can make your type fancy. And that's the impression it gives—someone trying to make their type look fancy because they don't know what else to do with it. When you let the computer add a shadow with the click of a button, you have no control over where the shadow goes or how thick it is, and most often it just looks cluttered and junky because of all the different parts of the letters in various layers. It creates an especially bad effect if the type is a script face.

Again, look around, try to put into words what other people have done to make their type stand out without resorting to using an outline and shadow.

Help! I can't swim!

11. Twelve-point type and auto leading

Just because the default is 12-point type with auto leading doesn't mean you have to use it. For most typefaces, 12-point is a tiny bit too large for body copy. Take a paragraph of 12-point text and set the same paragraph in 10, 11, or perhaps 10.5 point. Compare the two printed pieces; notice which one gives you a more professional, sophisticated impression. Add an extra 1 or 1.5 points of linespace (leading). Compare them again. What do you think?

12. Underline

This is a law: **never use the underline feature.** An underline means one thing: *italicize* this word. I know you were taught to underline titles of books, but that's because the typewriter (or your teacher) couldn't set italics. And *underlining italic text* is one of the most redundant things you can do in life. I know you sometimes underlined to emphasize a headline or a word, but that's because you didn't know how to make the type bolder or bigger or a different face. Now you know. Now you have no excuse.

Drawing a rule ("rule" means line) under text is very different from hitting the underline keystroke. When you draw a rule you have control over how thick it is, how long it is, and how far below the type it sits. But when you tell your computer to underline, the line bumps into the letters, obscures the descenders, is a clunky thickness, and looks dumb.

13. All caps

All caps are more difficult to read. That's just a fact: we recognize a word not only by its letters, but by the shape of the whole word. When text is in all caps, every word has the same shape so we have to go back to reading letter by letter.

All caps are fine sometimes, when you *consciously* choose to accept their lower readability because you need the look of all caps. But when you're setting headlines, subheads, lists in a parts directory, catalog entries, or other items that need to be skimmed and absorbed quickly, all are read more easily and quickly if they are in lowercase. If you use all caps because you want the words to stand out, or because it makes them appear larger and you think it's easier to read, THINK AGAIN. Find an alternate solution, such as **bold lowercase,** more space surrounding the text, **a different typeface,** a rule beneath, behind, or above the text.

And of course no one reading this book would ever put a font like Zapf Chancery in all caps. And outlined and shadowed. Score fifty-one points for yourself if you do. The capital letters in script faces are always more elaborate because they are meant as swash characters to introduce a word. When you set these froufrou letters in all caps, they bump into each other, overlap where they shouldn't, fit poorly together, and generally look stupid. Add the outline and shadow and you have the worst possible typography on earth, worse than any grunge type you may cringe at.

THE BLUES IS HARD TO LOSE.

Your score?

If you scored above three points, don't worry. Creating professional-level type is mainly a matter of becoming more aware of details. It usually doesn't take any more time to do it "right," and it is certainly not difficult to gain control over these details. If you scored less than three, then congratulations, and consider it your obligation to gently teach others the things you know.

I base my fashion taste on what doesn't itch.
Gilda Radner

Trends in Type
by John Tollett

Fifteen years ago, how many typesetters and typographic designers did you know on a first-name basis? And how many do you know today? I'm willing to bet my last, crumpled, 1980s vintage sheet of press type that *most* of the people you know have a better type selection at their finger tips than many professional typographers used to have in their shops. I'll do better than that. I'll bet my treasured, white-handled, tooth-marked x-acto knife that within the past hour or so, you've made a life-or-Helvetica decision.

Back when I was using that x-acto knife to burnish down that sheet of press type, if someone had asked me to bring them up to date on current type trends, I would have noted the revival of some dated faces like Cheltenham, or the popularity of extra-tight letter spacing in headlines. They probably would have looked at me and smirked, "Golly, I'm *so* impressed! Tell me (yawn) more."

But hold on to your digital hat. That was then and this is now. The technology of desktop and World Wide Web publishing has transformed the old graphics neighborhood into a much more exciting, innovative, and creative world. And that's why identifying trends is difficult . . . there's so much happening on such a steep curve of change that current trends don't have the opportunities that our ancestor trends had. But, hey, this is the digital era and if you want to make it as a trend, you're going to have to really wow us with your stuff.

For the sake of this discussion, let's say that *trends in type* refers to both *font design* (the look and feel of the individual characters of a font) and to *typographic design* (using type as the major visual element in layout and design.) This makes a huge category, but I nominate the following six entries as the most obvious candidates for trendom.

1. MOST CONTROVERSIAL TREND:

UGLY TYPE, LAWLESS DESIGN

This one really rocked the boat. If you haven't seen it, you've been spending too much time at the Helvetica User Group meetings. Some people think these ugly fonts are a fad that has started to fade. But if you look around, you'll realize that grunge type and lawless design is not only everywhere, it's so common that it doesn't shock us like it used to. Ugly fonts are not only outrageous by traditional standards, sometimes they range between barely legible and you-gotta-be-kidding-if-you-think-I-can-read-this. But g u e s s what else they are. They're interesting. Designers who are trying to get your attention, who are trying to convey a feeling with type (and some who know a trend when they see one), are using ugly fonts and ugly design. Ugly design abandons most things that are familiar to us such as consistent leading, symmetrical columns, reasonable contrast between words and Background, in favor of lines of type crashing into each other columns of type crashing into each other columns of type on top of each other,

words bleeding off the page and anything else that would terminate your employment in most places. There are some traditionalists who are getting close to marching through the streets with torches and pitchforks to round up grunge design before it destroys our typographic village. Some traditionalist aren't worried at all because it's laughable that such a ridiculous thing could have much influence. Uh oh. Look around you. mtv. espn. National magazines, national advertisers ... everyone is feeling the graphic influence of grunge. Like trends in fashion, designers take elements of what's happening in the most extreme cases and use them in more conservative ways. You'll see ugly fonts used in traditional layouts. I've used

some very stranGe fonts for some very conservative clients (a community college, a banK, and a magazine for cad engineers). Some designers prefer using traditional, classical typefaces in a grunge-inspired layout. Some do both. You Don't have to plunge into grunge, but it's really fun to get your feet wet.

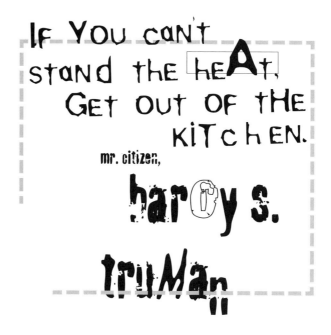

2. Most Amazing Trend: Special Effects Type

The first time I saw a designer stretching and squeezing type on a computer monitor, I knew my graphic life was going to change, but little did I know what magical changes they would be.

Some of the things you can do with type today aren't new. Dazzling effects were being created before desktop publishing, but mainly by those lucky enough to have giant budgets and lengthy production schedules. Most of us flipped through the design annuals of yesteryear and wondered how this was done or what genius did that? Who has that much time or budget? Fortunately, there was a digital daybreak on the horizon emblazoned with the motto: New Ballgame, Amigo!

Tired of flat type just lying there, staring at you? With software and software plug-ins available today you can transform your headline into a

piece of art, or at least an eye-stopping dynamic graphic. You can render a word or a sentence in 3D, rotate it, render it in color, and specify what direction the light is coming from and what color the light is. Change the color of the ambient light and map a texture to the surface of the type. Bevel the edge of the type. Create a soft drop-shadow that blends into the background color. Twirl, zig, zag, ripple, shatter, or vector warp your type. Shade the inside of the type with blends of color. You can do all this at your desktop in less time than it used to take you to find the phone number of some master hand-lettering expert.

The software tools for creating special effects are getting more powerful, more affordable, and easier to use, so this is a trend that is just becoming a way of life. The only designers jumping off this bandwagon are ones who are looking for the next big whatever. The next time one of these techniques jumps off the page at you, say hello to a trend.

3. Most Beautiful Trend: Rendered Type

I've separated this category from the previous one because this one is really a combination of illustration and typography. These are the kinds of typographic examples that *really* used to seem out of reach. How often were you going to hire photographers, illustrators, and retouch specialists just so you could have a snazzy looking headline? Forget it, Junior Art Director . . . use Garamond Bold and color it bright red. But now it's *everywhere*. It's everywhere because it's easy!

Type that's partially blended into a photograph or embossed onto a texture. Photomontages rendered on top of a headline. How about textures and effects that look photographic but were created from scratch on the computer, or patterns that have never even been created before? If you really want to dazzle 'em, this one's for you.

4. Most Obvious Trend: Abundance of Font Choices

For many years I felt that I was familiar with every typeface available. Even if some got past me, it was very seldom that I saw a typeface and didn't know its name or at least recognize it. And it was *guaranteed* that I knew every font available in my local area. Plus every style of press type available at the local art supply store. Here's another "that was then" pause. Now I can't even stay familiar with the fonts on my own computer, much less have a comprehensive idea of all the available fonts from the outside world. I was looking at a friend's type catalog recently and I didn't know one single font in the entire catalog. Everyone's on the font bandwagon. It's not just the large, professional type-setting houses buying fonts out there anymore . . . now it's millions of desktop publishers expressing their

individual and eclectic tastes. Traditional type designers are generating out new designs, both classical and grungy. New type design companies are springing up and making quite an impact. Freelance designers are designing fonts. Fonts are being designed specifically for the Internet and low-resolution monitors. I know a little girl named Scarlett who designed a font (named Scarlett) and I've seen it used in full color brochures from here to Europe. I've even seen fonts that look like they've been influenced by this seven-year-old designer. Fonts used to be very expensive. Now vendors practically give them away. As a matter of fact they do give them away. In addition to commercial font prices dropping tremendously, there's a large (and growing) collection of shareware and freeware fonts available. Don't plan on collecting them all unless you have a big hard drive with several terabytes of space.

You may argue that you'll never use or even see half of these fonts. That's probably true, but until the government limits type usage to Times and Helvetica, font creation is a runaway trend train.

SCARLETT DESIGNED THIS FONT WHEN SHE WAS SEVEN!

5. Most Fun Trend: Breaking the Rules

Breaking the rules of design. Big deal. "I do it everyday," you say. That's partly because the rules are fairly subjective and trying to agree on exactly what the rules are could cause a Holy Graphics War. Going out on a graphic limb or out on a design ledge is pretty common, even encouraged. The rules I'm talking about are the untouchable sacred cows of legibility and readability. If there's one rule that I made sure I *never* broke, it was this one: no matter how wild and unorthodox the design, you *had* to be able *at least* to read the copy. Ah, those were the good old days. Fortunately, not many designers are feeling compelled to carry their desktop creations this far. But on the other hand, there are enough people pushing the conventional legibility envelope (even normal, well-adjusted designers) that I'm proclaiming this an official recognizable trend. I know, I know . . . you're probably saying, "I'll believe it's a trend when *Robin Williams* designs a grungy type book." Oh, you poor, poor soul. You've got a lot of catching up to do.*

* *See* A Blip in the continuum *by Robin Williams, illustrated by John Tollett*

6. Most Important Trend: Typographic Independence

In the past, our design choices were limited. First, our font choices were limited to whatever choices our typesetter had made to include in her library. Her choices were usually the most mainstream, commercially acceptable, and popular font designs. Now, with the large commercial libraries, freeware, and shareware (and all of them available online), our choices are almost unlimited. If you think you're going to run out of choices, you can create your own font design.

Next, we were limited by time and budgets. Okay, those limitations are still there, but they've been minimized by our ability to experiment, create, and produce typographic design on our computers for a fraction of the time and money it used to take. The argument you still hear from the disappearing contingent of desktop critics is that computers just can't deliver the finesse that a type master can give you. I always wondered who those type masters were and why they never worked the midnight shift while my job was being set. My beloved x-acto knife saved a lot of typesetting jobs, but it can't compete anymore. So to the typesetter who once kicked me out of her office because I wanted her to reset some type: Game over, man.

Typographic Independence is here!

Future Trends

This is the exciting part. Some of our documents are no longer flat images of type and photographs fixed to a static page. With the advent of the World Wide Web, many documents are interactive and dynamic. A headline can animate while it moves around on the page; a logo can change into a headline with the click of the mouse; type can change colors or size; and 3D type can rotate or spin. While all this sounded futuristic a couple of years ago, it's becoming commonplace on the web. Certainly a future trend is more interactive type.

Another future trend is the design and usage of more fonts created specifically for display on computer monitors. The driving force for font technology up to this point has always been to optimize the output quality for publishing in the print media, but fonts designed for low-resolution web publishing will flourish and will influence print designers as well.

Web designers are limited to some degree by the technology available and by the speed with which most people can access web pages through their computers. As web browsers, programming languages, and the speed of Internet access improve, designers will have more freedom in web site design, and the creative possibilities will be more extensive than ever before, including the possibilities of what we can do with type. Look out.

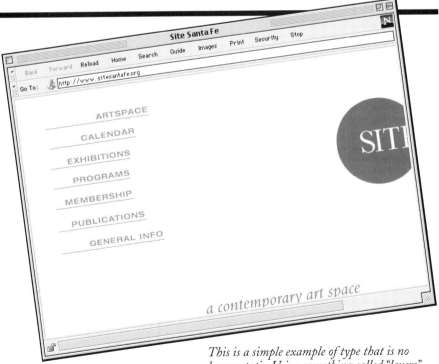

This is a simple example of type that is no longer static. Using something called "layers" on the web page, this logotype moves across the screen, as you can see on the opposite page.

So, in the near future, when the student intern in the cubicle down the hall is using some new holographic feature on a multi-dimensional, multimedia document, I'll just have one thing to say: "Go get your own x-acto knife, dude. This one's got sentimental value."

BE NOT

too tame neither,

but let your own discretion be your tutor;

suit the font to the word,

the word to the font...

paraphrased (forgive me) from
HAMLET, William Shakespeare

Other Info

In which there is important information regarding the fonts in this book, setting special characters, and several font utilities.

Font and Product Vendors

Font Vendors

The Beatty Collection
Hendersonville, NC
704.696.8316

Font Bureau
326 A Street, Suite 6c
Boston, MA 02110
617.423.8770
www.fontbureau.com

FontHaus Inc.
1375 Kings Highway East
Fairfield, CT 06430
800.942.9110
203.367.1993
203.367.1860 fax
www.fonthaus.com

Foster & Horton/FoHo Fonts
211 West Gutierrez Street, #3
Santa Barbara, CA 93101-3481
805.962.3964

GarageFonts
P.O. Box 3101
Del Mar, CA 92014
619.755.4761 phone and fax
www.garagefonts.com

Hoefler Type Foundry, Inc.
611 Broadway, Room 815
New York, NY 10012-2608
212.777.6640
www.typography.com

Adobe Studios
previously ImageClub Graphics
833 4th Avenue S.W.,
    Suite 800
Calgary, Alberta T2P 3T5
Canada
888.502.8393
403.294.3195
www.adobestudios.com

**International Typeface
Corporation (ITC)**
228 East 45th Street, 12th floor
New York, NY 10017
212.949.8072
www.itcfonts.com

LetterPerfect
526 First Avenue South,
 Suite 227
Seattle, WA 98104
800.929.1951
www.letterspace.com

PageStudio Graphics
3175 N. Price Road, #1050
Chandler, AZ 85224
602.839.2763

Plazm Media Cooperative
P.O. Box 2863
Portland, OR 97208-2863
503.222.6389
800.524.4944
www.plazm.com

Font Products
(Mac only)

**Adobe Type Reunion (ATR)
$39.99; upgrade $29.99**
*bundled with Adobe Type
Manager Deluxe, $79.99*
Adobe Systems, Inc.
345 Park Avenue
San Jose, CA 95110
408.536.6000
800.445.8787
www.adobe.com

TypeTamer
$59.95; download a free trial
Impossible Software, Inc.
Irvine, CA 92619-2710
714.479.4800
800.470.4801
www.impossible.com

WYSIWYG Menus
$129.95; upgrade is $29.95
Qualcomm, Inc.
www.nowutilities.com
*download a free trial
of the entire package*

KeyCap
from Big Rock Software, Inc.,
licensed to Adobe, found on
some Adobe CDs, such as
"Type on Call," and included
when you buy an expert set

**PopChar Pro
$39 by e-mail; $59 on disk**
Günter Blaschek
Uni Software Plus GmbH
Softwarepark Hagenberg
Haupstraße 99
A-4232 Hagenberg/Austria
www.unisoft.co.at/products/
popchar.html

Font Management Utilities

Adobe Type Manager Deluxe $69.99; upgrade $49.99
bundled with Adobe Type Reunion Deluxe (bundle is Mac only), $79.99
Adobe Systems, Inc.
345 Park Avenue
San Jose, CA 95110
408.536.6000
800.445.8787
www.adobe.com

Font Reserve $119.95 (Mac only)
DiamondSoft, Inc.
351 Jean Street
Mill Valley, CA 94941
415.381.3303
www.fontreserve.com

Page Layout Applications

Adobe PageMaker
Adobe Systems, Inc.
345 Park Avenue
San Jose, CA 95110
408.536.6000
800.445.8787
www.adobe.com

QuarkXPress
Quark, Inc.
P.O. Box 480787
Denver, CO 80248-9809
303.894.8888

Create your own typefaces, customize existing ones for your own use, and more with

Macromedia Fontographer

600 Townsend Street
San Francisco, CA 94103
415.252.2000
www.macromedia.com

Web sites

Chris MacGregor's Internet Type Foundry Index
This is an incredibly useful site for typophiles. Chris keeps up on who is doing what in the type world and works very hard to maintain this site so it benefits you. He provides a link to every type vendor in the world, plus information on many other aspects of type and a variety of resources. Tell Chris I said hello.
www.typeindex.com

Will-Harris House
Daniel Will-Harris provides another labor of love, the Will-Harris House, directed to people who care about type. You'll find articles, opinions, humor, and history here. You'll also find an interactive method for determining the most appropriate typeface for a job. Daniel is an expert on working with and using fonts on PCs. Tell Daniel and Toni I said hello.
www.will-harris.com

Typeface Samples

This is a list of the type-faces I used in this book. The initials preceding each type name refer to the vendor who sells the face. Many faces can be purchased from a number of vendors, but many of the really peculiar fonts are available only from the original source.

Some type vendors' names, phone numbers, and addresses are on the preceding page. Almost all can be found at Chris MacGregor's web site, mentioned on the previous page (**www.typeindex.com**). These initials refer to the following vendors:

A Adobe System, Inc.
IC Adobe Studios (previously Image Club Graphics)
CC Carter & Cone
FH FontHaus Inc.
FS FontShop USA
GF Garage Fonts
MT Monotype Typography, Inc.
RB Richard Beatty Designs
P Plazm Media Cooperative
PS Page Studio Graphics
SH Shareware (go to **www.shareware.com**)

A Aachen Bold, 170
FH Amoebia Rain, 42, 115
A Antique Olive Black, 128, 190
Antique Olive Compact, 46
Antique Olive Light, 129, 198
Antique Olive Nord, 128, 129, 171
Antique Olive Roman, 45, 48
SH Bad Copy, 26, 96, 138
A Bedrock, 27
A Belwe Condensed, 152
Belwe Light, 34, 152
Belwe Medium, 129
A Bembo, 28, 119
IC Bernhard Bold Condensed, 138, 153
Bernhard Modern, 34, 45, 48, 74, 128, 138, 156, 184
CC Big Caslon, 99
FH Birds, 163
A Bodoni, 23
A Bookman, 181
FH Carpenter, 170
A Caslon, 22, 99, 153, 156, 157
Caslon Bold, 157
SH Cheap Signage Standard, 42
GF Chicken, 30, 32, 171
IC Chilada Dos, 27
A Clarendon, 24, 171, 181, 182
Clarendon Bold, 182
Clarendon Light, 181, 182
A Courier, 46

FH Decon Struct Bold, 156
Decon Struct Medium, 152
FS Dirty Four, 30
Dirty One, 153
A Dorchester, 50
FS Dynamoe, 200
P Erosive Plain, 186
A Eurostile, 93, 190
Eurostile Bold all caps, 111
Eurostile Bold Cond., 75, 124, 153
Eurostile Bold Ext. Two, 96, 124, 141, 157
Eurostile Condensed, 93
Eurostile Demi, 57, 58, 59, 60, 64, 65, 71, 143, 157
Eurostile Extended, 93
SH Eviscerate, 208
A ExPonto Multiple Master and alternates, 27, 74, 96, 152, 156
IC Fantasia (EPS caps), 153
A Fette Fraktur, 32, 170
A Flyer Condensed, 25
Flyer ExtraBlack Condensed, 156
A Formata Bold, 190
Formata Light, 39
Formata Medium, 25
Formata Regular, 35, 133
IC Fragile, 201
A Franklin Gothic Condensed, 95
Franklin Gothic Heavy, 170
SH Garamond Backwards Light, 102
A Garamond Book, 34, 94, 183
Garamond Light, 22, 35
Garamond Light Condensed, 95

Ornaments on these pages are from the Toulouse–Lautrec set of fonts from Monotype.

Appendix C
Font Utilities

This section contains some information about utilities available to help you with your typefaces, as well as charts of the special characters and how to type them. For Windows users, there is not much else available besides what you see in this section. For Macintosh users, you might want to check out another book of mine, *How to Boss Your Fonts Around, Second Edition,* for more information on a variety of other utilities available to make your font menu easier to use, plus guidelines on how to organize and store your fonts, and how to manage them.

Where to find what for the Macintosh:

Where to find what for Windows:

PopChar Lite ▪ Mac

PopChar Lite is a freeware piece of software, a little control panel. Drop it onto your System Folder, restart, and then you can access it. Choose a font in your document, press on the tiny symbol that appears in your menu bar, and you get this box that displays all the characters in the font. Slide over the one you want, let go, and that character appears in your document. The keys to create that character are displayed in the upper-right corner.

PopChar Pro ▪ Mac

PopChar Pro is the shareware version of the free version shown above. In this version you can choose various layouts for the characters. Notice the characters in this dialog box (shown below) are more organized. You can also disconnect the window so it floats around your Desktop while you work, and you can zip it down into this tiny little piece that unzips whenever you need it:

KeyCap ▪ Mac

This is not the Apple Key Caps utility that comes with your Macintosh. This is Adobe's utility called KeyCap that usually comes on a disk when you buy an expert set, or you might find it on any of your other Adobe disks. Just double-click on the icon (shown below), then choose a font from the menu. All of the characters in that font will appear in a nice window as shown below. Click any character to see it in the enlargement window. From the File menu, you can choose to "Print Fonts…." Select any number of fonts from your list and KeyCap will print a separate chart like this for each one.

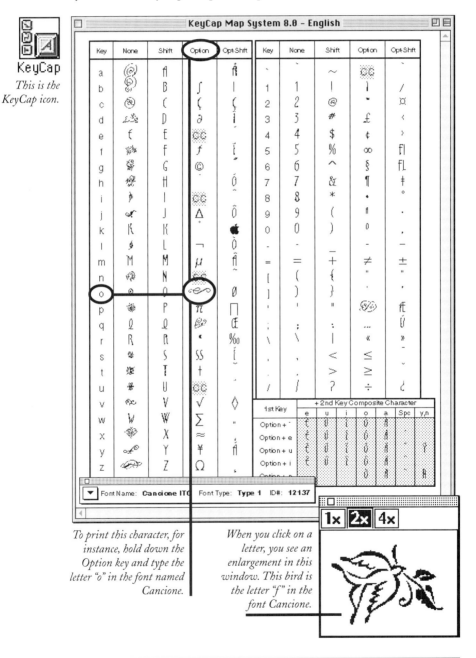

KeyCap

*This is the
KeyCap icon.*

*To print this character, for
instance, hold down the
Option key and type the
letter "o" in the font named
Cancione.*

*When you click on a
letter, you see an
enlargement in this
window. This bird is
the letter "f" in the
font Cancione.*

Adobe Type Manager Deluxe ∙ Macintosh

Every Macintosh needs a regular version of Adobe Type Manager (ATM) so your Post-Script fonts appear clean and smooth on the screen, and so they print clean and smooth to non-PostScript (inexpensive) printers. The Deluxe version of ATM goes a big step further—it allows you to open only the fonts you need at the moment, and to create "sets" of fonts so you can open or close all the fonts that belong to a project at once. See **www.adobe.com**

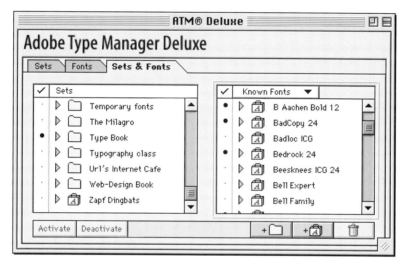

Font Reserve ∙ Macintosh

Font Reserve from DiamondSoft is another great program that allows you to open just the fonts you want, instead of all of them you own. You still need a regular version of ATM on your Mac, but if you decide to use Font Reserve, do not install the Deluxe version of ATM! See their site at **www.fontreserve.com**

Special Characters ▪ Mac

You can type these characters in any application on the Mac—word processing, page layout, spreadsheets, paint programs, draw programs, etc. To type: *hold down* the modifier key noted (Option, Command, and/or Shift), then *tap* the character key *once*. If some of these characters don't show up when you print, you may need to check your Page Setup dialog box and make sure the option that says something like "Include symbol font for special characters" is turned on.

Character	Type it this way	What is it?
'	Option]	opening single quote
'	Option Shift]	apostrophe, closing single quote
"	Option [	opening double quote
"	Option Shift [	closing double quote
‹	Option Shift 3	opening single French quote (guillemets)
›	Option Shift 4	closing single French quote (guillemets)
«	Option \ (backslash)	opening double French quote (guillemets)
»	Option Shift \	closing double French quote (guillemets)
–	Option - (hyphen)	en dash
—	Option Shift - (hyphen)	em dash
…	Option ;	ellipsis
®	Option r	registration symbol
©	Option g	copyright symbol
™	Option 2	trademark symbol
•	Option 8	bullet
·	Option Shift 9	raised period
·	Option h	really raised period, or a dot
°	Option Shift 8	degree symbol
/	Option Shift 1	fraction bar (slash: /; fraction bar: ⁄)
fi	Option Shift 5	ligature for the f-and-i combination
fl	Option Shift 6	ligature for the f-and-l combination
œ	Option q	lowercase oe diphthong, or ligature
Œ	Option Shift Q	uppercase OE diphthong, or ligature
æ	Option '	lowercase ae diphthong, or ligature
Æ	Option Shift '	uppercase AE diphthong, or ligature
¶	Option 7	paragraph symbol
§	Option 6	section symbol
†	Option t	dagger
‡	Option Shift 7	double dagger
	Option Shift V	diamond, lozenge
¢	Option 4 (the dollar sign)	U.S. cent
£	Option 3 (pound sign: #)	British pound sterling
¥	Option y (y for yen)	Japanese yen
¤	Option Shift 2	general currency symbol

¿	Option Shift ?	inverted question mark
¡	Option !	inverted exclamation point
ß	Option s	Beta, or German double s (ss)
ø	Option o	lowercase letter o with slash
Ø	Option Shift O	uppercase letter O with slash
	Option =	does-not-equal sign
	Option x	approximately-equals sign
	Option < *(above the comma)*	less-than-or-equal-to sign
	Option > *(above the period)*	greater-than-or-equal-to sign
±	Option Shift +	plus-or-minus sign
÷	Option /	division sign
	Optoin v	radical sign; square root symbol
f	Option f	function symbol or freeze
	Option b	integral symbol
	Option 5	infinity symbol
¬	Option l *(the letter el)*	logical NOT, negation symbol
‰	Option Shift R	salinity symbol
ı	Option Shift B	dotless i
ª	Option 9	feminine ordinal indicator
º	Option 0 *(zero)*	masculine ordinal indicator
	Option d	lowercase delta
	Option j	uppercase delta
	Option p	lowercase pi
	Option Shift P	uppercase pi
μ	Option m	lowercase mu
	Option w	uppercase sigma; summation
	Option z	uppercase omega
^	Option Shift i	circumflex*
~	Option Shift n	tilde*
¯	Option Shift , *(comma)*	macron*
·	Option h	dot*
°	Option k	ring*

* These accent marks cannot be placed above a letter, as can the accent marks below.

Accent marks directly over the letters

~	Option n	as in ñ in piñata	tilde
´	Option e	as in é in résumé	acute
`	Option ` *(to left of number 1)*	as in à in voilà	grave
¨	Option u	as in ï in naïve	diaeresis
^	Option i		circumflex

To type the letter with the accent mark above it, do this:
>   Hold down the Option key and type the key noted in this chart (such as Option n). Nothing will appear to happen!
>   Let go of the Option key, then type the character you want (n).
>   The character will appear with the accent mark directly over it.

Adobe PageMaker ▪ Mac

These are the shortcuts you can use in Adobe PageMaker, in addition to setting all of
the special characters shown on the previous two pages.

Non-breaking spaces

These spaces of varying width do not break; that is, the computer does not see them as word spaces
at the end of a line, so if a non-breaking space is between two words, those two words will never separate.
Also use these spaces to make quick indents, consistent spacing in a line of items, etc.

em space	(width of point size)	Command Shift M
en space	(half of an em space)	Command Shift N
thin space	(quarter of an em space)	Command Shift T
non-breaking regular space		Option Spacebar

Special hyphens

Type the **discretionary hyphen** between syllables in a word when you want to hyphenate a word at the end of a
line, but you want the hyphen to disappear if the text gets edited. You can also type this invisible character at
the beginning of a word, and that word will never hyphenate.

- (discretionary hyphen)   (v6.5) Command Shift Hyphen   (v6 or v5) Command Hyphen

Type the **non–word-breaking hyphen** between hyphenated words so those words will never separate, even at
the end of a line. It will look just like a regular hyphen. You might want to use it in phone numbers.

- (non–word-breaking hyphen)   Command Option Hyphen

Kerning

Position insertion point between two characters, or select a range of characters. Then:

amount	delete space	add space
.001 (thousands of an em)	type in negative amount in the control palette (-.003)	type in positive amount in the control palette (.004)
.01 (hundredths of an em)	Command Delete	Command Shift Delete
.04 (quarter of an em)	Option Delete	Option Shift Delete
Remove all kerning	Select the text, then press Command Option K	

Baseline shift

The baseline shift amount in the control palette (shown below) is determined by the amount you set in the
General Preferences (shown farther below). Hold down the Shift key (in version 6, use the Option key) to
nudge by ten times the amount set in Preferences. That is, if your nudge amount is set at 1 point, Shift-
nudge would move items in 10-point increments.

Before you baseline shift, be sure to first select the characters you want to move.

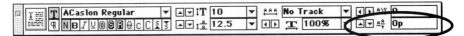

*Either enter an amount here in this box,
or click the up and down arrow keys.*

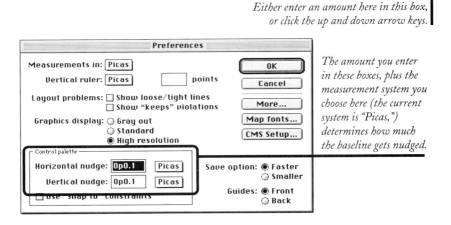

*The amount you enter
in these boxes, plus the
measurement system you
choose here (the current
system is "Picas,")
determines how much
the baseline gets nudged.*

QuarkXPress ▪ Mac

These are the shortcuts you can use in QuarkXPress on the Macintosh, in addition to setting all of the special characters shown on pages 220–221.

Non-breaking spaces
These spaces do not break; that is, the computer does not see them as word spaces at the end of a line, so if a non-breaking space is between two words, those two words will never separate.

en space (half of an em space)   Command Option Spacebar

to make an en space that **does** break, use Option Spacebar

non-breaking regular space   Command 5 (from the keyboard, not the numeric keypad)

Discretionary hyphens
Type the **discretionary hyphen** between syllables in a word when you want to hyphenate a word at the end of a line, but you want the hyphen to disappear if the text gets edited. You can also type this invisible character at the beginning of a word, and that word will never hyphenate.

- (discretionary hyphen)   Command Hyphen

Type the **non–word-breaking hyphen** between hyphenated words so those words will never separate, even at the end of a line. It will look just like a regular hyphen. You might want to use it in phone numbers.

- (non–word-breaking hyphen)   Command =

Kerning
Position insertion point between two characters, or select a range of characters. If you select a range of characters, then the command "Kern" turns into "Track." It's doing the same thing.

amount	delete space	add space
.005 (¹/₂₀₀ of an em) (10 units)	Command Shift [OR type in negative amount in the control palette or Character dialog box	Command Shift] OR type in positive amount in the control palette or Character dialog box
.05 (¹/₂₀ of an em) (1 unit)	Command Shift Option [OR type in negative amount in the control palette or Character dialog box	Command Shift Option] OR type in positive amount in the control palette or Character dialog box

Either select the numbers right here and type in your own amount, or click on the arrow keys to add or delete space in increments of 10.

Baseline shift
Before you baseline shift, be sure to first select the characters you want to move.

up one point   Command Option Shift + *(plus key on keyboard, not keypad)*

down one point   Command Option Shift - *(hyphen key on keyboard, not keypad)*

up or down in smaller increments   use the Character dialog box, from the Style menu

Character Map ▪ Windows

The font utility Character Map is installed along with Windows. In Windows 95, you'll probably find it in your Start menu, under Programs, then Accessories. The Character Map is shown below.

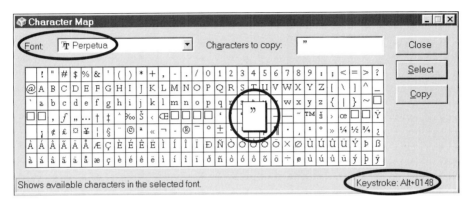

Choose a font from the menu. Every one of its characters will appear. Hold your left mouse button down and slide your pointer over the characters—each one will show up enlarged, as shown above.

Double-click on any character and it will be added to the little box at the top, "Characters to copy." You can then click the "Copy" button, return to your document, and paste that character (or as many characters as were in the "Characters to copy" edit box) into your document. Remember, they will paste in wherever the insertion point is flashing.

Also note the bottom-right corner: Character Map tells you the code to insert that character directly into your document. Remember, you have to hold the Alt key down while you type those four numbers, using the numeric keypad (not the numbers across the top of your keyboard!).

ANSI chart ▪ Windows

The following characters can usually be added into most word processing and page layout documents by using the ANSI code. To type these codes, hold down the Alt key and type the four numbers (always a zero first) from the numeric keypad, then let go of the Alt key. Do not use the numbers across the top of your keyboard! You must use the numeric keypad on the right side of your keyboard.

If you use PageMaker or QuarkXPress, check the following pages for the shortcuts to type these special characters without having to type the ANSI code. Also check the Character Map, as described on the previous page.

If these don't work in your software, check your manual. Some other software packages also provide their own shortcuts for these characters. You might also want to see *The PC is not a typewriter.*

Character	Type this code	What is it?
'	Alt 0145	opening single quote
'	Alt 0146	closing single quote
"	Alt 0147	opening double quote
"	Alt 0148	closing double quote
•	Alt 0149	bullet
–	Alt 0150	en dash
—	Alt 0151	em dash
…	Alt 0133	ellipsis
™	Alt 0153	trademark symbol
©	Alt 0169	copyright symbol
®	Alt 0174	registration mark
¢	Alt 0162	cents symbol
£	Alt 0163	British pound sterling
¥	Alt 0165	Japanese yen
é	Alt 0233	e with acute accent
ñ	Alt 0241	n with tilde

Adobe PageMaker ■ ■ ■ ■ ■

PageMaker includes built-in shortcuts for some of the most commonly used special characters so you don't have to type the Alt codes (but you can always use any of the Alt codes if you choose in PageMaker). In addition, there is information below about other special PageMaker features that help in the typographic world.

Character	Type it this way	What is it?
'	Alt [	opening single quote
'	Alt]	apostrophe, closing single quote
"	Alt Shift [	opening double quote
"	Alt Shift]	closing double quote
–	Alt - *(hyphen)*	en dash
—	Alt Shift - *(hyphen)*	em dash
®	Alt r	registration symbol
©	Alt g	copyright symbol
•	Alt 8	bullet
§	Alt 6	section symbol

Non-breaking spaces
These spaces of varying width do not break; that is, the computer does not see them as word spaces at the end of a line, so if a non-breaking space is between two words, those two words will never separate. Also use these spaces to make quick indents, consistent spacing in a line of items, etc.

em space	(width of point size)	Control Shift M
en space	(half of an em space)	Control Shift N
thin space	(quarter of an em space)	Control Shift T
non-breaking regular space		Control Alt Spacebar OR Control Shift H

Special hyphens
Type the **discretionary hyphen** between syllables in a word when you want to hyphenate a word at the end of a line, but you want the hyphen to disappear if the text gets edited. You can also type this invisible character at the beginning of a word, and that word will never hyphenate.

- (discretionary hyphen)   (v6.5) Control Shift Hyphen   (v6 or v5) Control Hyphen

Type the **non–word-breaking hyphen** between hyphenated words so those words will never separate, even at the end of a line. It will look just like a regular hyphen. You might want to use it in phone numbers.

- (non–word-breaking hyphen)   Control Alt Hyphen

Kerning
Position insertion point between two characters, or select a range of characters. Then:

amount		delete space	add space
.001	(thousands of an em)	type in negative amount in the control palette (-.003)	type in positive amount in the control palette (.007)
.01	(hundredths of an em)	Control Alt LeftArrow	Control Alt RightArrow
.04	(quarter of an em)	Alt LeftArrow OR Control Backspace	Alt RightArrow OR Control Shift Backspace
Remove all kerning		Select text, press Control Alt K	

■ ■ ■ ■ ■ Windows

Baseline shift

The baseline shift amount in the control palette (shown below) is determined by the amount you set in the General Preferences (shown farther below). Hold down the Shift key to nudge by ten times the amount set in Preferences. That is, if your nudge amount is set at 1 point, Shift-nudge would move items in 10-point increments.

Before you baseline shift, be sure to first select the characters you want to move.

Either enter an amount here in this box, or click the up and down arrow keys.

Preferences

Measurements in: Picas

Vertical ruler: Picas ___ points

Layout problems: ☐ Show loose/tight lines
☐ Show "keeps" violations

Graphics display: ○ Gray out
◉ Standard
○ High resolution

Control palette
Horizontal nudge: 0p.1 Picas
Vertical nudge: 0p.1 Picas
☐ Use "Snap to" constraints

OK
Cancel

More...
Map fonts...
CMS setup...

Save option: ◉ Faster
○ Smaller

Guides: ◉ Front
○ Back

The amount you enter in these boxes, plus the measurement system you choose here (the current system is "Picas,") determines how much the baseline gets nudged.

QuarkXPress ▪ Windows

QuarkXPress includes built-in shortcuts for some of the most commonly used special characters so you don't have to type the Alt codes (but you can always use any of the Alt codes if you choose). In addition, there is information below about other special Quark-XPress features that help in the typographic world.

Non-breaking spaces
These spaces do not break; that is, the computer does not see them as word spaces at the end of a line, so if a non-breaking space is between two words, those two words will never separate.

en space (half of an em space)   Control Alt Shift 6

to make an en space that **does** break, use Control Shift 6

non-breaking regular space   Control Spacebar

Discretionary hyphens
Type the **discretionary hyphen** between syllables in a word when you want to hyphenate a word at the end of a line, but you want the hyphen to disappear if the text gets edited. You can also type this invisible character at the beginning of a word, and that word will never hyphenate.

- (discretionary hyphen)   Control Hyphen

Type the **non–word-breaking hyphen** between hyphenated words so those words will never separate, even at the end of a line. It will look just like a regular hyphen. You might want to use it in phone numbers.

- (non–word-breaking hyphen)   Control =

Kerning
Position insertion point between two characters, or select a range of characters. If you select a range of characters, then the command "Kern" turns into "Track." It's doing the same thing.

amount	delete space	add space
.005 ($^1/_{200}$ of an em)	Control Shift [	Control Shift]
(10 units)	OR type in negative amount in the measurements palette or Character dialog box	OR type in positive amount in the measurements palette or Character dialog box
.05 ($^1/_{20}$ of an em)	Control Shift Alt [	Control Shift Alt]
(1 unit)	OR type in negative amount in the measurements palette or Character dialog box	OR type in positive amount in the measurements palette or Character dialog box

| X: 0.708" | W: 3.021" | △ 0° | ⇧ ☐ | ☰☰☰ | Helvetica | ☐ 18 pt ☐ |
| Y: 0.806" | H: 2.875" | Cols: 1 | ⇔ 0.008 | ☰☰ PBIUW⧉◉⑤Kκ | |

Either select the numbers right here and type in your own amount, or click on the arrow keys to add or delete space in increments of 10.

Baseline shift
Before you baseline shift, be sure to first select the characters you want to move.

up one point   Control Alt Shift)

down one point   Control Alt Shift (

up or down in smaller increments   use the Character dialog box, from the Style menu

Adobe Type Manager Deluxe ▪ Windows

Why would you want to use Adobe Type Manager Deluxe on your Windows machine since your TrueType fonts look just fine on the screen? One good reason is to change your type menu **from this:**   **to this:**

Adobe Type Manager Deluxe not only installs PostScript fonts for you, but it manages those PostScript fonts *and* your existing or new TrueType fonts. You can open just the typefaces you are using in a project, instead of having every typeface you own open all the time. You can view and print a sample of any typeface (as shown to the left), and you can customize what that sample says. If you want to make new Multiple Masters instances, you must install Adobe Type Manager Deluxe. I don't know why anyone would want to be without it.

— continued next page

ATM Deluxe ■ Windows ■ continued

This is a quick overview of how you can use ATM Deluxe to create new sets, add new fonts, or change the sample text. Be sure to read the small and excellent manual.

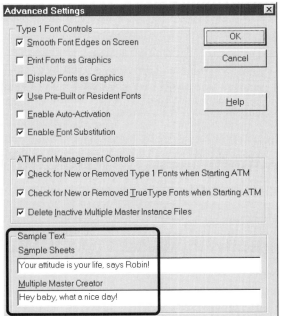

Click "Add Fonts" to make new sets (explained below), add fonts to existing sets, or to install fonts from a removable disk onto your hard disk.

You can create "sets" of fonts, then turn those sets on or off. You can turn any number of sets on (limited only by how much memory you have in your computer).

In the example above, I have just made a new set called "Robin's fonts," shown on the left side. On the right side, two fonts are selected. I can click the "Add" button to add those two fonts to the selected set ("Robin's fonts"), or I can simply drag them over to the set folder on the left and drop them in. A checkmark next to the set folder means those fonts in that set are loaded.

You can change the text you see in the sample (as shown on the opposite page).

Click the "Settings" tab in the main dialog box, then click the "Advanced..." button. At the bottom of this dialog box, select the existing text and type in whatever you want. Whatever you type into "Sample Sheets" will appear in the large sample pages. Whatever you type into "Multiple Master Creator" will appear when you create new Multiple Master instances (shown on the following page).

ATM Deluxe ■ Windows ■ Multiple Masters

Here are very brief directions on how to create new multiple master instances. You should really read the manual also, to understand the whole picture and all the details.

1. Open Adobe Type Manager Deluxe. Click the tab "Add Fonts." From "Source," choose "Create Multiple Masters." You will get the dialog box shown below.

2. Choose a multiple master typeface from "Multiple Master Base Font." Use the slider bars to create the look you want. Click the "Bold" or "Italic" checkboxes to make it bold or italic. (The text you see in the sample box is the text you can change from the Advanced Settings dialog box, shown on the previous page.)

3. When you like the typeface you created, click the "Add" button and the new instance (plus its base font) will be added to the list of faces to open on the left. If you select a set before you click the "Add" button, the new instance will be added directly into that set. If the checkmark is on, that new typeface will now be in the font menu in your application.

Index

About the Author

I live on several acres of piñon forest just south of Santa Fe, New Mexico. I'm still a single mom of three kids, three dogs, but no more cats. I'm online often, but I hardly ever read my e-mail. Someday, though, I will answer every one of those 4,273 messages that are still in my box. You'll be surprised. I've written a lot of other books, and I do a lot of workshops and seminars around the country. **www.ratz.com**

About this Book

I created this book in Adobe PageMaker 6.5, which I love. I designed the pages, wrote the text, did the production, and produced the index and table of contents in PageMaker.

The cover was designed, illustrated, and produced by John Tollett, an incredibly talented and nice man. He used Adobe Photoshop 4 and PageMaker 6.5

Main fonts in the book: Dorchester Script for the chapter headings; Eurostile Bold Condensed for the headings and subheads; Caslon expert set for the body copy. The list of over 115 fonts sprinkled throughout the book is on pages 214–215. Cover fonts: Minister from Adobe Systems, and Bodega Sans, by Greg Thompson.